JUST CATS

DEDICATION

To Carol
who sent the "Get Well"
card that prompted
this story

Just Cats

by

Sheila Caselberg

BREWIN BOOKS

First published February 1990 by
K.A.F. Brewin Books, Studley, Warks. B80 7LG

Cover design and all other drawings by
Christine Cater

ISBN 0 947731 64 4

Typeset in Pyramid 12pt.
and made and printed in Great Britain
by Supaprint (Redditch) Ltd.
Redditch. Worcs.

CONTENTS

LIST OF ILLUSTRATIONS

CHAPTER 1

FELIX

I was sitting in the straight-backed chair of a hospital bedroom waiting anxiously for the consultant to visit me. I was nervous; I tried to read, my eyes moved along the pages of the book in my hand oblivious of the printed words, my thoughts elsewhere. I gazed round the flower filled room and admired the 'Get Well' cards from so many friends, and my eyes were drawn back to one which I had placed in such a prominent position that I could not fail to constantly admire it - a black cat sitting in the middle of a garden with flowers and trees in the background. The cat was called Felix, one of my nieces had sent it to me; it reminded me of the black cat waiting at home. A sharp knock on the door brought me back to the present; soon the piercing eyes of the consultant were upon me as words of wisdom and advice poured out; I must cease all active pursuits and have a period of enforced rest. 'How long' was my first question. A vague reply.

'It could be weeks or even months'.

I was stunned. I led a very active life, too active it appeared. Dozens of thoughts flashed through my mind, there was much to consider and to re-organize; I reached for the telephone and dialled my husband. He was at once reassuring yet firm that I should come to terms with the news. I was to be allowed home in a week's time, things began to look brighter; I settled back in the chair and looked more keenly at the card of Felix, gradually I recalled the many cats I had encountered; then an idea began to form, I would refresh my memory by writing about them.

'Relax, try to enjoy the remainder of your stay in hospital', I told myself. The room was more than comfortable. I had a colour television set mounted on the wall, a

1

radio and telephone by my side.   At the push of a button I could summon help or order refreshments.   The bed was adjustable, I could alter the height of the whole bed or change the angle of the sloping pillows to put myself in a sitting position.   There were comfortable chairs and a writing table.   Such luxury was to be enjoyed to the full. I haven't mentioned the food;   well, the food was unquestionably delicious and delightfully presented, it could not be faulted.   In fact, the hospital was run like a first class hotel.   The staff courteous, helpful and efficient, from the porter who delivered the newspapers to the nurses who administered one's needs.   I was beginning to feel better already.   I would ask Peter to bring in some foolscap paper, in the meantime, I might as well make a few notes.

How should I begin?   There had been many individual feline characters in my life, some more pleasing than others, both in habit and appearance;   why not write about all of them, the good and the bad, the beautiful and the ugly, the beggars and the thieves.   I would start with Feckless for she is the Queen Bee of the household, now a mature lady of uncertain years.   To call her a lady is a little misleading - she had been neutered before she made friends with my husband and me.   Why we were the chosen ones I do not know, but Feckless knew, and so she will feature most in this little story.

CHAPTER 2

THE INTERLOPER

We had moved house, into a smaller one almost a stone's throw from our previous home. Before taking up residence I had many times noticed a black cat sitting on the garden fence, observing me whilst I washed down kitchen tiles and generally made preparations that are so necessary prior to a removal. This, I considered to be a lucky omen. Now, in this house we have a room we call a sun lounge; it is a glass enclosed extension added on to the main lounge which we have furnished with comfortable chairs from which we admire the garden. It is also our custom to take meals in the extension during the summer months.

One wet summer's day Peter and I were sitting in the aforementioned room when there appeared at the glass door a very wet, dishevelled, small, black cat. We had no cat of our own at this time - in fact not for some years had any feline decorated our hearth, no cat stretched full length in order to gain maximum warmth from whatever source of heat was available. But, we had befriended a beautiful, black female cat belonging to neighbours at our former address. She came to us whenever her owners went on holiday, in spite of arrangements being made for someone to feed and attend to her daily needs. Her name was Sheba; Sheba had bewitched us and let it be known that we were to be her guardians whenever necessary. You've guessed correctly, we thought Sheba had discovered our new home. You may think was it not possible to recognize her? Well, this little cat at the door was wet, and wet fur flattens, distorting features. We opened the door - that was inevitable and in she came, no hesitation, tail in the air and started to purr. The food and drink we offered were greedily accepted. Then we telephoned our former neighbours. No, Sheba was asleep on one of their beds. So who was our visitor? When the rain ceased we insisted she left.

I must digress here to write a little about Sheba. I have already said she was small, black and quite beautiful. Being an unneutered female she had several litters, proving herself to be an excellent mother. Several times she brought one special litter of three over the fence to show me; little balls of fluff barely able to balance; climbing the garden fence must have been a major operation. I was sure one would topple into a pond we had by the fence, so out came a roll of wire netting and the pond was duly covered. Sheba loved climbing, she was often to be seen climbing the sloping roof of her house to enter through a window. Would she teach the little ones this method of entry? If she did they all survived the ordeal. She also had an endearing habit of pretending to run away having once caught your attention, then stopping abruptly to roll over and with a melting gaze demand to be petted. This little trick always worked.

It was Sheba's custom to perch on a stone post in her front garden and show off her beauty to all who passed, everyone had to stop to stroke Sheba, even those in a hurry. Children could just reach her stretching up standing on toes. She dazzled her admirers.

Sadly, some time after we had moved we learned of her death; one day she was just not quick enough in crossing the road and was run over. So many people enquired about the missing Sheba that a notice was displayed reporting her death. It spared the grief to her owners of verbally recounting her unhappy end. We grieved too, when we read the sad little notice. One of her kittens remained with Sheba's owners but it never developed Sheba's unique personality.

On the day of the removal from our previous house, a young grey cat appeared and wandered round looking into every room whilst the furniture was being loaded. It mewed piteously, gave the impression of being starved, and would not be turned away. With the house now empty and time to leave there seemed no alternative but to take the intruder with us. Peter vaguely remembered seeing two similar cats in a street nearby whom he thought belonged to a colleague of his at the BBC. A telephone call proved him right. We discovered that the owner's garden backed onto the garden of our new home, but strangely that little grey cat never once visited us in our new abode.

I must return to the black cat now often to be found sitting on one of our comfortable chairs in the sun lounge. We had traced the owner, who lived only three doors away, and discovered the reason why the cat left home so much; she had recently acquired a young kitten, Feckless, our interloper, took exception to this, determined to find a new home for herself she had selected us to be her new guardians. I don't know how she came to be called Feckless; regretfully I never asked. The Concise Oxford Dictionary gives the meaning of the word as feeble, futile, inefficient. Perhaps she was the smallest of a litter. The word can also mean indifferent, and Feckless can certainly be indifferent. She is not a beautiful cat. Her slightly Oriental look suggests some Siamese blood in her; she is not large enough for it to be Burmese. Her ears are large and her head small. Feckless's most attractive feature is her eyes; they are bright green and can register anticipation, anger, indignation or jealousy, according to her mood. When she has persuaded someone to stroke her under the chin she half closes the eyes giving a penetrating, enquiring look rather than a look of pleasure. Some cats are more expressive than others; Feckless falls into the category of very expressive. She walks with one front leg bent slightly inwards, making her appear bandy. Her other gaits are more graceful. She has short hair, the black being tinged with brown down the inside of both front legs.

Having established her right to one of our armchairs, she soon extended her territory to the garden and made friends with a young black and white feline neighbour called Bosey. They would spend hours frolicking together, playing catch me, rolling over in mock fights and chasing each other up one of the tall cypresses that grace the garden. Feckless, the bolder of the two, was able to knock her companion over and dash away before he could pick himself up. He would appear crestfallen, pretend to attend to some important grooming then jumping like a gamboling lamb would return for more games and more punishment.

We have a very pretty garden; it was landscaped by

previous owners. A raised rockery curves away from a narrow path; three tall cypresses are off-set in different parts of the lawn underplanted with perennial flowers encircling the trees. There are attractive azaleas at the bottom of the garden next to lilac trees. Rhododendrons and masses of flowering shrubs lead the eye down another side; a huge beech tree adds shade to a sunny part of the garden and a magnificent magnolia greets early summer with it's delightful blossom. A Japanese maple, smaller pine trees and an ancient, purple wisteria all add beauty to the garden. It is a private garden with lovely trees which in no way overwhelm the scene. The lawn is not perfect for the squirrels are constantly digging away, sometimes finding nuts, sometimes hiding nuts; their activities adding interest to the changing seasons. We plant the borders with annuals trying to remember which plants did well. Neither of us has green fingers, but we are determined this lovely garden will not be neglected.

One day we noticed a 'For Sale' sign in Feckless's front garden. This was an unexpected disappointment for we had become very attached to the wayward cat and the prospect of loosing our young intruder did not appeal to us. However, her mistress had other ideas; she asked if we would consider adopting Feckless as she feared the small cat would not settle when they moved. We agreed wholeheartedly. Feckless who had first entered our household by virtue of mistaken identity, now officially belonged to us. That is, if cats ever belong to anyone! And so our lives changed; we belonged to Feckless; we were there to satisfy her every whim; to feed and amuse her, dance attendance on her and to cease our activities if they interfered with whatever she wanted at that precise moment. Little did we know when we agreed so readily to take her in, that in due course she would have us both at her beck and call.

"A lovely bird bath cum sun dial"

CHAPTER 3

EARLY RECOLLECTIONS

My first childhood recollection of any pet belonging to the family is being aware of my father carrying a wicker cat basket along a crowded railway platform, endeavouring to find the guard's van into which to deposit the protesting animal. How the other members of the family boarded the train I do not recollect. However, I do remember making frequent visits to the guard's van, accompanied by my brother and sister. I doubt if our attempts to calm the cat were successful, but the trips were a diversion on a long rail journey. I can't remember what we called the cat, or it's colour or size, but I must have been fond of the animal for I pestered my mother as to whether it would settle in our new home, and she replied, 'We'll put butter on his paws then he won't stray.' I am not sure if she did put butter on the cat's paws but not one of our cats tried to find it's old home.

My father was a Naval Constructor, and the nature of his work meant he spent three or four years working at the Admiralty, followed by a similar spell at a Naval Dockyard - then back to the Admiralty, so many journeys were made transporting cats by rail. When my father finally bought a motor-car we were without a household pet. This was remedied shortly after he left the Dockyard at Barrow-in-Furness to return to the Admiralty; my parents had chosen a house in Surrey as our new home, but it was to hold sad memories; the lovely family cat they bought for us was killed by a neighbour's dog. It was a shattering experience for young children and we could not be consoled; any thoughts of obtaining another cat were abandoned.

During that period of my childhood lost animals singled me out as a companion. I remember one foggy night an Airedale followed me when I was walking home after attending night school. My exhaustive attempts to send him away

8

had no effect.   I arrived home tired and cold.   The dog too looked a pathetic sight, shaggy coat dripping from the damp fog.   There was a collar round his neck giving his address and my kind father got the car out of the garage and drove the Airedale home; by this time the fog was more dense but in no way did my father show signs of displeasure, such was his good nature, combined with a sympathetic understanding of his young daughter.   Foggy days and nights were common-place - the days of smoke-less zones had not come into force, but it was safe for teenage girls to attend night classes and walk home alone.   I was improving my German conversation and enjoying the experience immensely, no doubt because the class spent much time singing German songs!   The period was about a year before the outbreak of the Second World war; at that time any interest in the German language or the country itself was not viewed with suspicion.   Stray cats were a different problem; any cat or kitten that tried to attach itself to me had to be sternly discouraged for the neighbours still had their wayward dog.   No cat was safe whilst he lived next door to us.

The saddest memory of my time in Surrey was the death of my father.   He lost his life in the submarine "Thetis" which sank off Liverpool Bay in June, 1939.   My mother never recovered from those nightmare days of attempted rescue that led to hope then despair, when it was painfully obvious no more could be rescued.   Only four men out of the one hundred and three aboard her, survived.   The Admiralty advised my mother to leave the precinct of London with the threat of war hanging in the air, so my shattered mother gathered up her family and belongings and took us north to Hest Bank on the fringe of the Lake District.   There a new life began.

CHAPTER 4

THE SCRATCHING POLE

Feckless, we soon discovered, delights in scratching household objects; furniture, chairs, books, anything that takes her fancy. The snagging of upholstery displeases me most and Feckless knows this by the tone of my voice in reprimanding her. She started a game; she would sneak into the lounge, climb onto a chair, give it a quick scratch, jump down and hurry away, usually to race upstairs making as much noise as a heavy battalion on the move. She hoped I would chase her. In an effort to break this unpleasant habit I bought a scratching pole; a rather expensive and elaborate affair. The pole was entwined with thick rope; swinging from the side of the pole was a soft ball, impregnated with some special substance reputed to appeal to cats. It had the opposite effect on Feckless; she declined to go near the contraption. We attempted to demonstrate the use of the scratching pole by holding her paws on it and gently drawing them up and down. She knew only too well the function of the pole and merely shook a paw in it's direction as she walked away with a contemptuous look on her face. Peter and I knocked the ball slowly backwards and forwards hoping the swinging action would tempt Feckless to join in. As she idly watched us she seemed to be thinking 'Let others play with the ball it seems to amuse them.'

The scratching pole was returned to the pet shop and exchanged for a cat bed. A nice, soft, fabric cat basket with a low front. Would Feckless use it? No! The basket was not to her liking. In recent months I have bought her a bean bag, and this she does like. Oh, it took a little time. We first introduced Feckless to the bean bag by placing it in front of an electric fire and putting her on it; she likes to warm herself in front of any fire; stretching her legs and at the same time opening and closing her claws, revelling in the warmth of the fire on her body.   At first she was suspicious of the new bed, the beans shifted and made her unsteady, she couldn't get comfortable.

'I don't think this is such a good idea,' Peter conjectured.

'Give her time,' I said, and put the bed in a corner of the lounge on top of an old record player.   Some days later Feckless wasn't to be found anywhere in the house.   It was cold; we knew she wasn't outside, then we discovered her, curled up on her bean bag; she had made a well in the middle of the bed, sunk into it and the contents had moulded to her shape making a snug little place to hide.   It has her seal of approval, so the bean bag is moved from room to room; to a bedroom for the night, the dining-room when we eat, the lounge at the end of the day.

The problem of the scratching has not been solved, except that Peter has placed a piece of wood on the corner of a bedroom wardrobe which she was in the habit of scratching.   The wardrobe became so dilapidated I'd contemplated throwing it out, now with the piece of wood in place she pops into the room for a quick scratch whenever she wishes.

Another of her bad habits is to jump on top of the books I keep on the landing in an opened shelved bookcase and proceed to scratch.   Her claws are so sharp that little piles of paper dust often accumulate on the books, sometimes dropping behind the shelves to form small heaps on the carpet.   To stop this I've put magazines on the top shelf and these are scratched instead of the books although she is less inclined to attack them now she has got the piece of wood on the wardrobe.

Chairs in the dining-room have to be protected with arm covers and antimacassars.   It is always my intention to whip these off whenever anyone calls, but invariably friends come unannounced and are seated in chairs with all their coloured array.   Needless to say, Feckless can jump under the covers and scratch the chairs from the rear.   We now possess two new armchairs in the dining-room and a new suite in the lounge!   And I've threatened to have her claws removed!

"She knew only too well the function of the pole"

CHAPTER 5

COUNTRY CATS

Our house in the village of Hest Bank was called "Beech-field", so named because of the tall beech trees which were a main feature of the three acres surrounding the house. Tall poplar trees flanked the stables and also formed a coppice by the garage. The rear of the house faced west and the sun-sets were breath-taking; I still get a thrill as I recall the glowing red sky as we watched the sun disappear into Morecambe Bay. When the wind blew in from the sea it rustled the leaves of the poplar trees which seemed to sigh and whisper as they swayed in the breeze. The air was fresh and slowly wounds began to heal. Part of the healing process was provided by a grey pony which my mother bought for my brother and me; now snow white in his older years, aptly called Snowball for he was also very rotund. I had the most enjoyment with Snowball for my brother was away at boarding school and my sister soon returned to Surrey.

The first pet to join the household was a female, black cat, whom we unoriginally called Blackie because of her colour; unbeknown to us Blackie was pregnant. She was soon joined by an old English sheepdog called Gyp. Gyp was a youngster, eighteen months old; she had proved to be an unwilling worker on the farm where she was bred so her farming owners gave her to me; but Gyp soon discov-ered the sheep and cattle in the fields adjoining our land and much to that farmer's annoyance would round them up. She was not a true old English sheepdog for she possessed a tail, and I for one was delighted; I would never have seen her excited tail thump the ground, or be held high if on the trail of something interesting. One of her joys was to follow me when I rode out on Snowball; this could be a disadvan-tage for I might wish to ride near the railway line, or go down to the sea-shore, which meant crossing a main road and Gyp was not exactly traffic trained. If I left Beechfield without her and she caught me up I just hadn't the heart to send her home, her pleasure in having found me was so overwhelming.

I mention Gyp because she displayed the most amazing gentleness with Blackie's kittens; these kittens were born in a cardboard box in the kitchen. I don't remember exactly how many kittens Blackie had, although I was present when the first was born. I think she may have had four or five. Like most newborn kittens Blackie's were not beautiful; kittens are born blind and remain so for between five to ten days, but they are able to suckle in a very short time. Blackie proved a dutiful mother and soon decided a cardboard box was not a suitable home for her off-spring. She selected a cupboard next to an open fire-place in the sitting-room; when Gyp observed Blackie moving her kittens she decided to assist her; very gently she picked one up in her mouth and conveyed the kitten to it's new home, then she repeated the process whilst Blackie remained in the cupboard; none was harmed and soon all were safely installed in the new, dark hiding place. I watched Gyp make several journeys with the kittens so there must have been at least four. This gentle behaviour of Gyp's may have been because she had experienced motherhood before she joined us and when she was only a puppy herself. We were lucky in finding homes for all the kittens and in due course my mother had Blackie neutered.

A recent heavy snowfall accompanied by high drifting has reminded me how much Blackie loved to play in the snow; her black coat would show up in sharp contrast against the white all around her; she would jump into the snow actually playing with it, showing her pleasure in a child-like manner. The cold never seemed to bother her; unlike Feckless, who even in her younger days walked very gingerly across a snow covered garden. Nowadays, one look outside standing on the doorstep sniffing the air is enough to send Feckless back indoors to the warmth of a radiator.

Two stray, wild, young farmyard cats next found their way to Beechfield; a home was made for them in the loft above the stables. The cats were both black with white markings; one had four white paws, the other four white stockings, the white stretching all the way up his legs.   I called them White Paws and Puss-in-Boots.   In the early days when I went to feed them it was necessary to wear leather gauntlet gloves for they flew at my hands with open claws so eager were they to get to the food.   The stables had started off as stalls which we had had converted into two loose boxes;   they were housed within a building and a huge loft ran the whole length of the block.   One of the windows had a small pane of glass missing and the two cats used this as their means of entry and exit.   White Paws would sit for hours on a bench by the open window waiting for me to visit the stables;   if I happened to enter unobserved I would hear the sound of scurrying feet across the floor above, then they would tumble over each other in their haste to descend the ladder leading from the loft.   Gyp, also, loved to go up into the loft, coming down the open tread steps was a different matter and very difficult for a dog.

It took some time for the wild cats to learn to trust me; with frequent meals they gradually became less energetic in their efforts to grab the food from my hands.   It was point- less to take it in a cat bowl as I learned to my cost in the early days, for that was soon sent flying.   I devised various methods of transporting the food to them - no tinned delicacies in those war time days - so cooked offal, fish heads and any left overs were carried in newspaper.

When I gave the pony his daily groom the two cats would play under his feet;   one day, Puss-in-Boots, the more mischievous of the two, jumped onto Snowball's back and started kneading his paws in the pony's coat;   each time I lifted him off he returned.   Snowball didn't object and I do believe the cat thought he was assisting me in the grooming; it became a ritual.   Not long afterwards the now tame cats started sneaking into the house;   from the kitchen they wandered into the morning-room and discovered the warmth of a coal fire.   Blackie tolerated them and so they joined the indoor brigade and were allowed to stay.

Peace indoors did not reign long;   our lives were dis- rupted by two young evacuees from London;   (evacuees from war torn London), brothers of about nine and eleven years of age.   They tormented the cats, teased and provoked them.

We tried extra hard to interest the boys in country life but all to no avail, they hated life in the country and became more disruptive. My mother felt unable to discipline them as they were away from their own home and parents and these were difficult times for everyone. Speculating that it might help the boys to settle if they saw their parents my mother invited them to spend a holiday with us. That was a disaster; the boys behaved atrociously after they left. The cats fled the house whenever the brothers entered; I spent more time working outside than was necessary; we grew all our vegetables in never ending rows; and cultivated tomatoes in two huge greenhouses with the help of an elderly gardener who came to us once a week. I also kept hens, having reared fifty Rhode Island Reds from day old chicks.

The chicks had to be fed every few hours when first hatched. To reach the chicken house I had to walk through an orchard to get to the field the hut was in; the first time I went out to feed the chicks in the early hours of the morning it was pitch dark and quite eerie. I had forgotten Snowball was in the same field as the chicks and he managed to scare me dreadfully by coming to the chicken house door when I was inside. It was some time before I realized that the strange noises and movement outside were being made by the pony.

Before long my mother's health deteriorated; finally the young boys were found accommodation in a town house where they were much happier and we had an Army Officer billeted on us.

I was excused 'call up' into one of the Women's Services because of my mother's ill-health, instead I was allowed to work at the Canadian Army Treasury, whose Headquarters had been transferred to England from Ottawa; I worked in the Personnel Department in converted offices in the King's Arms Hotel in Lancaster. My day started early for the chickens had to be fed before the cats and the household, then I had a long walk to the nearest bus stop - services being curtailed with petrol in short supply; our own vehicle was

16

laid up on blocks in the garage, drained of water with an empty petrol tank. There were many days when I was too exhausted to ride the pony when I finished work. Then my farming friends who had given Gyp to me suggested I turn the pony out to grass on their land, and this I did; my brother and I making visits to fuss and ride Snowball whenever possible in his school holidays.

After the evacuees left Beechfield the cats resumed a fairly normal existence, they were good at adapting to different situations and there was much to occupy them; hunting expeditions for field mice, birds to stalk and chase. Not one of them caught a rat and we were troubled by these rodents around the hen huts; some country folk came along with ferrets and terriers and made a great deal of noise and caught nothing. Finally our very handsome Rhode Island Red cockerel shamed all of us by demonstrating that he could deal with the situation and protect his hens by catching and killing several of the largest rats I had ever seen. I should add that the rats were only interested in the food put out for the poultry.

A friend lent me a shot gun loaded with spray shot. 'You're bound to shoot one,' he gaily informed me. Early one morning, having locked the chickens in the hen hut, I put out some food in a trough and positioned myself behind a tree. I hadn't long to wait, in no time a very fat rat appeared at the trough and started eating the corn; I took aim and fired, the noise startled me and the act of firing the shot nearly sent me flying for I wasn't ready for the rebound action of the gun. I looked in the direction of the feed trough; the rat had disappeared, but it wasn't lying dead on the ground, it was obvious I had missed. Somewhat mortified I returned the gun to it's knowledgeable owner.

When peace was declared it was time to leave our country retreat; my brother was now studying in London, my sister already there, so a return south was thought practical. The cats were adopted by the new owners of our house; Gyp the old English sheepdog was the only pet to accompany us. It was heart breaking to leave the cats; but they had only known country life, it didn't seem fair to move them to an entirely new environment; to a small garden compared with their freedom in the country, to the hazards of motor traffic, the hustle and bustle of town life; and on reflection I am sure it was the right decision.

We acquired a second Blackie to ease our grief. She had the sharpness akin to a London Cockney. It did not take her long to learn how to use our door knocker. She would stand on her hind legs and pull the knocker then let go only to repeat the act. Many times she gave one or other of us quite a shock to discover no-one at the door, until we observed a black cat pushing in, even then it was not until someone witnessed her actually using the knocker that we believed she could be so clever. But I must return to our very clever present black cat, Feckless.

CHAPTER 6

MORE ABOUT FECKLESS

Peter's sister Sonia was staying with us. 'Why don't you get a bird table for the garden?' she announced one day. Sonia is interested in all things connected with gardens and her keen eye had noted something missing in ours.

'What a good idea,' I replied, we put nuts out for the squirrels and feed the birds in the winter, but we just hadn't thought of a bird table. We spent the next few days visiting all the garden centres close to hand; then we drove into the country calling at garden nurseries. We wanted something a little unusual, something that would age well and blend in with the garden. Finally we stumbled across an elderly stonemason who designed and cast garden ornaments. We chose a lovely bird bath cum sun dial. The sun dial would serve as the table. It was made in two parts and although the base was exceedingly heavy we heaved it into the car boot and drove home. 'Where should we site it?' was the next question.

'Not dead centre in the lawn,' Sonia said, 'you want to see it from several windows.' Peter moved the heavy object whilst Sonia and I went from room to room calling out if it was in sight. Having settled on a position I suddenly remembered we hadn't checked if it could be seen from the kitchen. 'I would like to see the bird table from the kitchen,' I said apologetically. 'After all I spend a lot of time in the kitchen.' Peter moved it once more, with success. We can view the bird bath from two bedroom windows, the lounge, sun lounge and the kitchen. It has given us many happy moments watching the birds drinking or having a bath. 'There's a jay on the sun dial,' one of us would call, or 'Can you see the squirrel eating a nut?' We have some relatively tame squirrels in the garden; sometimes they enter the sun lounge in search of a nut or two. In those early days Feckless would chase them considering their presence an intrusion. I don't encourage the squirrels to enter the house; I prefer them to confine their antics to the garden. Feckless loved to stalk a squirrel then chase it up a tree. The squirrel would race along one of the branches then jump from one tree to another whilst Feckless would be left sitting at the bottom of the tree wondering how the squirrel had disappeared.

It did not take Feckless long to understand our retiring to bed preparations; the ritual of tidying the room before leaving it; the locking of the doors; food to be put into her bowl in case of night starvation, and so forth. Each of these tasks would be performed with Feckless following us around, and when all were completed she would scamper up the stairs ahead of us. If, by chance, we decided to stay up later than our usual time, perhaps to watch an interesting programme on the television, or to listen to the radio, Feckless made it quite plainly understood that she disapproved, and indicated her impatience by strutting back and forth and then jumping on and off one of our laps and generally making a nuisance of herself. Similarly, if either of us chanced to be reading a book or a newspaper she would put herself between the book and the person reading, or try to sit on the newspaper. In the end her command had to be obeyed. This display of displeasure also reared it's head whenever we listened to taped music played on a record player; I think her previous owner, who was a musician, may have recorded the music playing of some of her pupils, much to Feckless's distaste. She certainly dislikes all music coming from a recording machine, but will accept music when heard on the radio or the television.

I think quite a few cats like to disrupt letter writing; many times Feckless has sent a pen scrawling across a page necessitating that page to be re-written or explained; she sits down on the notepaper and demands to be made a fuss of; no amount of verbal admonishment will move her. 'Will you move Feckless!' one of us calls out, but it's no good she has to be picked up and placed somewhere else, usually this doesn't work for she is back in a few minutes attacking the pen and paper. Likewise, if the telephone rings Feckless is there to join in the conversation, walking round whatever furniture the telephone rests on, desperately doing her best to prevent any form of conversation taking place; one is so distracted by her performance that concentration is difficult - the more so if the call is an important one.

Another tantalizing habit of Feckless's is her delight in sitting for hours underneath the motor-car.   On warm days she prefers the bonnet; but when she is underneath the car and we want her indoors she becomes very stubborn, pretends we are not there by ignoring us completely and refuses to move.   I think she likes to watch the world go by under the comparative safety of the stationary vehicle.

Not many summers ago we had a spate of car thefts and property stolen from motor cars in the neighbourhood.   At about 11 o'clock one warm night Feckless decided to go out; now, if she chooses such a late hour to leave the house during the summer months Peter and I know it will be no good planning to retire for at least another hour.   On this partic-ular night, after a suitable time had elapsed, I armed myself with a torch and began looking for Feckless.   There seemed many more cars than usual left out in the road as I began my search under them - then I remembered the car thefts and thought my actions looked too suspicious to continue searching in this manner.   Peter said 'I'll get the car out of the garage she may come and sit under it.'   He had just closed the garage doors when she appeared as suddenly as the Cheshire Cat in Alice's Adventures in Wonderland, and we were able to go to bed.   You may think 'why don't they leave the cat out all night?' or, 'Have they no cat flap?'   The answer to the latter is, no, we have no cat flap into the house, and we are apprehensive about leaving Feckless out all night because our neighbourhood is bothered by urban foxes; but more about foxes later.

"Feckless loved to stalk a squirrel"

CHAPTER 7

STABLE CATS

I keep a Thoroughbred chestnut mare at livery in the country; my love of horses since my first pony, Snowball, has not diminished and since Peter shares this interest too, many hours are spent each day at the stables thus giving me the opportunity of observing the stable cats.

My association with Alcott Farm, the livery yard where I keep my horse, goes back over ten years, when I took a bay mare to be stabled with the young couple who had just opened their farm as a Hunter, Point-to-Point livery yard; some beef cattle and a few free range hens were also part of the establishment. The first cat I noticed was a huge tabby named Francis after a young relative, he was soon joined by kittens, Starsky and Hutch, (the television series Starsky and Hutch was running at the time.) One kitten, Starsky was mostly black with a white bib, the other a light tabby. Starsky is there to-day, still a little shy, but very tolerant of being picked up by small children and carried around with tiny hands clutching him tightly. He enjoys being stroked and can be quite vocal. His companion, Hutch, disappeared many years ago, his fate unknown. He might have been lost to a fox, he was the smaller of the two, and certainly foxes are plentiful there for they plundered the poultry until John and Jane decided enough was enough and did not replace them; they had made every effort to keep the hens in their quarters at night, but foxes are cunning animals and they won the battle. It was not an uncommon sight to see a hen fly up onto a stable door and hop over the other side; if you entered a little later it was not unusual to find an egg had been laid in the manger; the horses quite liked these visits for they enjoyed eating an egg or two. My own horse would leave traces of egg-shell in her manger or sometimes a broken egg, if she had eaten enough. Wherever there is farm fodder about there are sure to be rats; in an effort to control these pests two more cats were acquired - Charles and Diana. The young daughters of the house were given the task of finding suitable names and as this was the time of the engagement of Prince Charles to Diana Spencer they became known as Charles and Diana; both grey and white tabbies. I find it difficult to distinguish them apart but Peter informs me that Di has a little white under her chin and she delights in getting into the car if a door is left open, invariably leaving muddy paw marks everywhere revealing we've had a visitor.

After one particularly long session at the stables; we had shampooed my mare's coat ready for a show, washed her tail and she was all ready to have her mane plaited when we decided it was time for a break, time to eat the sandwiches I had taken along - sardine sandwiches which are Peter's favourite. I went to the car to get the picnic ready, 'Peter' I called, 'come and see what's happened to our lunch!' One of us had left the hatch door open and through this Diana had entered, found the sandwiches, torn open the parcel and scattered pieces of bread in all directions, having first eaten the filling!

Charles and Diana are both good hunters, but, alas, they also enjoy catching young birds and much time is spent trying to save the fledglings, mostly housesparrows, who's parents build their nests under the tiled roof of the stables. How can one teach farm cats that it is perfectly all right to kill rodents but not to hunt birds? The cats spend hours sitting quietly on the roof tops, where they can hear the sparrows quarrelling, waiting for one to hop out.

When kittens both Charles and Diana loved nothing better than to follow one of us into the tack room, and using the lowest saddle rack as a platform the kitten would leap onto a human shoulder with claws wide open; this hurt considerably, there would be shrieks of 'Don't Di,' or 'Get down Charlie,' but the kitten would have wrapped itself firmly round one's neck quite determined not to let go. The unfortunate victim was forced to seek assistance from whoever chanced to be passing. The kitten, purring loudly, would not object to being lifted off and made a fuss of by someone else.

My present mare, whose stable name is Millie, is allergic to dust and in order to alleviate this allergy we have her bedded down on paper, which we prepare ourselves at home putting newspaper through a shredding machine. This is a tiresome, time consuming process. It is possible to buy dust extracted paper but it makes it an expensive form of bedding. I do not think John would care to use paper in all his stables as this form of bedding necessitates more work in mucking out the stable, and in windy weather it tends to blow all over the yard. But it does make a nice, clean, warm bed, which the cats were not slow to discover and Di, Charlie or even Starsky often can be found curled up in a corner. It is a pleasing sight to see a horse lower his head and sniff a welcome to a cat which has just alighted on it's stable door. Cats are not afraid of horses and quickly learn to keep out of the way of flying hooves.

Occasionally a strange cat will appear at the farm and seek shelter in the hay in the barn. The home cats allow the intruder to stay for there is plenty of space and when in the hay a cat is well hidden. After a week or so the stranger may move on. The farm cats do not appear to fight amongst each other; they play, and they certainly play with the dogs on the farm, especially the young King Charles spaniel, Heidi; she is often to be seen having a boxing match with Charles or is it Diana? And in turn Heidi delights in tormenting Winston, the huge Bernese mountain dog. An elderly Jack Russell makes up the trio, Sadie, and when the weather is cold both Sadie and Heidi sit on Winston's tail for warmth; when he decides to wander off Heidi grabs hold of the tail in her mouth; she really holds hard and is pulled along until the huge dog stops to reprimand the small spaniel. He is very tolerant with the children too, allowing them to ride on his back. I once saw Heidi with a dead squirrel in her mouth; it was a young one, but whether she actually caught it I am not at all sure. I suspect one of the cats killed it then having got tired of playing with the rodent abandoned the dead animal. Heidi likes to follow the horses when they are ridden out; this is not encouraged for she was once picked up by a stranger in a motor-car and would have disappeared forever had she not managed to escape and run home.

Some years ago Whiskey, a black and white collie was

part of the farmyard scene; a sweet tempered bitch, she managed to get a leg broken whilst running beside a race horse which was being exercised in one of the fields; she didn't turn quickly enough on a bend. The leg mended and Whiskey went on to live to a ripe old age, although a little rheumatic.

There is always plenty to observe at the stables, horses to be exercised, perhaps taken over some of the cross-country jumps or shown to a potential buyer. Occasionally a vet is called out and a horse trotted up and down the yard while observant eyes are alert to spot any lameness; the hours pass quickly, then suddenly we are aware of the time and decide we must return home to see what our cats are doing. Yes, cats, for Feckless has been joined by two companions.

"Lowers his head to greet a cat"

CHAPTER 8

TWO TOM-CATS

Poorly Puss is a long haired, brown/black and white cat with a sweet face and beautiful yellow eyes. There is obviously some Persian in him. He can look pathetic and appealing at the same time, and he has been around nearly as long as Feckless, therefore, his age is not exactly known. One theory about him is that he got left behind in error when someone moved in the vicinity taking a young litter with them; he was subsequently fed by more than one household and lived a nomad life. He ruled the local cat kingdom for he was un-neutered and he put each cat in it's place with a sharp cuff across the ears or something even more severe if one strayed into his territory. He befriended Bosey (who featured early on playing with Feckless) and Bosey's owners named the stray tom-cat Poorly Puss because he was a poor little puss; they fed him alongside Bosey; but they moved away taking Bosey with them, consequently Poorly Puss became more dishevelled and uncared for as he continued to propagate the neighbourhood. One spring his coat was in a terrible state; huge lumps of matted fur hung loosely about him and no amount of grooming on my part made any difference. I could not disengage the matted hair, although I was able to cut away some with scissors. There was no alternative but to visit our local veterinary surgeon; Poorly Puss under-went a general anaesthetic to have the matted fur removed and the coat freed from all it's tangles. We took back a very sore cat indeed; in fact so much hair had been removed from his head that a young boy in the neighbour-hood remarked that he looked like a monk. When the tenderness had eased I started the daily task of combing the cat and he began to look very handsome indeed.

There now entered upon the scene a second tom-cat - an oddly marked black and white short haired cat - he was hungry and had sneaked into the house through the back door in search of food; we put some out for him, Feckless did not see him as a threat for he was a frightened cat and only made lightening visits. We left food in a bowl and put it on the back door step; gradually he became a little bolder, entered the house again and raided the pedal bin in the kitchen looking for scraps, for he was a scavenger. We made enquiries about this odd looking piebald cat, whom I referred to as Tom. It turned out to be the old story, someone had left the district only this time to move into a flat, they had left behind two cats. One was adopted by a neighbour, the other, Tom, was left to fend for himself. Peter and I decided to keep Tom and let him sleep in the boiler house, which is outside; but first we had to gain Tom's confidence, so we began by feeding him in this newly appointed sleeping place which Peter had made alterations to so the cat could enter easily, giving him enough room to squeeze in. While we were building up this confidence Tom encountered Poorly Puss who had ventured into the rear garden - the rear garden Tom considered his territory - no violence was used in that first encounter, just a great deal of vocal noise followed by a very slow retreat by Poorly Puss. This way of escaping unscathed is quite a spectacle to watch; it looks like a film being played in extremely slow motion, and it takes a long time for the moving cat to walk away. We were to witness this many times; on occasion Tom had to steal away if he chanced to arrive at a place which Poorly Puss had chosen to settle down in, and the roles would constantly be reversed.

We decided the time had come to have Tom neutered, he was now sleeping in a snug box in the warmth of the boiler house. I am pleased to say that the operation did not change his independent character, nor did it make him over fat. He is still wary, especially of strangers, and if I have a duster or a broom in my hand when he comes trotting along his immediate reaction is to take flight; this makes me assume that someone at sometime in his young life has chased him with these articles.

Peter, meanwhile, had provided Poorly Puss with a box to shelter in under a rhododendron bush in the garden at the front of the house next to the front door; Poorly Puss used this and would come out to greet us whenever he heard the car enter the drive. We always fed him by the front door but in wet weather he was allowed into the porch; sometimes he even ventured into the house and would stay a short while sitting in the hall. He still visited the neighbours and all his old haunts, and I continued to groom him; fortunately he loved having his coat brushed and combed so I was able to keep him looking fairly spruce. But his courting activities made him very thin and something had to be done to restrict the local cat population. Peter and I discussed the situation. After giving it some thought Peter said 'it wouldn't be right to have him neutered unless we are prepared to take full responsibility for him.'

'But we can't let him sleep in the house,' I answered, 'Feckless might leave as she did when her former owner acquired a kitten.' We let the matter rest for a day or two.

Feckless's means of entry into the house was through a spare bedroom window at the rear; she would climb up the sloping glass roof of the sun lounge, which was a tricky operation for she then had to jump through the window, but Tom soon learned this way of entry and one day we found Tom sitting on one end of a bed whilst Feckless sat at the other. This would not do; the inside of the house was Feckless's domain. After that little encounter the window remained closed.

Peter returned to the question of having Poorly Puss neutered or not. 'We could make a bed for him in the garage,' he suggested 'and I could fix a cat flap in the garage door.' This seemed a good idea to which I wholeheartedly agreed, and I went off to telephone the surgery, having first made sure none of the neighbours objected, for several people fed him and we didn't want to step in if someone had another idea.

In a very short time Poorly Puss's appearance changed. He began to wash and groom himself; his coat became silky and shone; he put on weight; he was less aggressive, in fact, he became very affectionate, so much so that he would roll over when spoken to, it was hard to resist tickling his tummy. Now we are greeted by three cats whenever we return to the house, however, only two enter by the front door, Feckless and Poorly Puss; Tom, knowing his place, rushes round to the back door - tradesmen's entrance for him - nevertheless they all end up in the kitchen.   At this stage Poorly Puss is the boss and Tom the underdog.   Feckless reigns as Queen.

I have just returned from a visit to the veterinary surgery with Tom.   He wasn't waiting on the doorstep when we got up this morning, which was unusual for Tom, so we searched the garden but couldn't find him.   He didn't appear when we called his name; thinking he had been fed elsewhere I carried on with my household chores.   At lunch time he was on the fence.   Calling his name I invited him in; he scrambled down and entered the house.   It was obvious something was wrong; he didn't want to eat or drink; he just sat looking very uncomfortable, whilst saliva ran out of his mouth.   I put him in a cat bed on a chair and left him to rest.   Several times in the afternoon I looked in at the unwell cat, there didn't appear to be any improvement so I tele- phoned the vet and arranged to take him to the evening surgery.   Tom was running a temperature and his respiration was quick.   The vet took one look in his mouth and confirmed he had a very inflamed throat and gums.   Poor Tom, no wonder he couldn't eat.   After an antibiotic injection we brought him home; he is to be on a course of drugs for five days.   Now we must wait and see if he has infected Feckless or Poorly Puss.   Being older than Tom they might be immune to the infection having built up some resistance.   There are so many different strains of cat influenza it is impossible for vaccines to give protection against all of them.

Now I must write about Feckless's disappearance, for shortly after officially adopting the two tom-cats Feckless disappeared.

"Gradually he became a little bolder"

CHAPTER 9

THE MISSING FECKLESS

It was Father's Day - June 19th - not that we celebrated it in any particular way, but it was a lovely hot June Sunday and I well remember the garden had to be watered. We made our usual journey to the stables early in the morning on account of the heat; we both rode Millie in what is known as the hill field; acres of undulating ground with banks and natural jumps. The mare was quite a handful; she is a typical chestnut, Thoroughbred mare, excitable and scatty. In the heat I soon tired so Peter took over. He is a much stronger rider than I am and is undetered by any out of control over excited gallop. One would imagine the horse would tire, uphill work in hot, humid conditions, but not so; Millie was enjoying herself, and at the top of the hill there was a welcome breeze. Peter paused to get his breath back; I remained seated on a log under the cool umbrella of an elm tree and watched the pair silhouetted on the skyline. I idly wondered if Feckless would be there to greet us on our return; we had let her out very early that morning and she was no-where about when we left, which was a little unusual; meanwhile, Millie had had her fun; Peter walked her down the steep hill. Back in the stable yard we washed the sweat off her steaming body then turned the mare into one of the fields to graze and drove home.

Tom and Poorly Puss were waiting, no Feckless. 'I expect she's sleeping in some shady spot,' I said, not sounding too convinced. 'Shall we have an early lunch then potter about in the garden?' Peter nodded his agreement, then set about putting out sun loungers; Feckless would often sit under a chair in the garden, it gave her both shade and security. We ate alfresco talking in louder tones than necessary in a vain hope to lure her out of any hiding place, then we made a pretence of weeding the rockery and the borders and finally sank into the chairs exhausted. Evening came and we watered the garden calling her name as we moved from one area to another; occasionally Tom appeared, followed by Poorly Puss. Darkness fell and we were still calling her; she had never been away so long. Reluctantly, Peter put the car in the garage and we went to bed.

An early rise Monday morning brought no Feckless to the door. The outlook was grim. Where was she? Had she strayed from home because of our attention to Tom and Poorly Puss? An even worse thought, had she found herself another home? I called on friends and neighbours enquiring if they had seen her, and returned home empty handed and saddened. I busied myself typing out 'lost' notices which I delivered to houses further afield. 'Would you please look in your garage or garden shed to see if a stray black cat has got shut in?' the notice read. I left one at thirty houses or more and knocked on the door whenever I noticed someone at home.

It was again hot and sunny; we postponed a visit to the stables until the cool of the evening; there was still no sign of Feckless when we returned. By now it was hard to mention her name to each other; we both assumed she had been hit by a motor vehicle and had crawled away to die in some lonely place; if this was so we should never know her fate. Tossing in bed that night I thought of the time we had gone on holiday a few years after Feckless had joined us. We had left her in the capable hands of a kind neighbour who had offered to feed and look after her whilst we spent a short break in Ibiza. The flight was an early morning one and it was still barely daylight when Peter got the car out of the garage for the drive to the airport. We had intended to let Feckless out as we left, the neighbour would feed her again later, but Feckless managed to sneak out of the house whilst Peter was putting the suitcases into the car, nothing would entice her back and she slipped away in the half light. All the way to the airport Peter constantly repeated 'Did she get into the garage?; we haven't left a garage key with Margaret!'

This fear of Feckless spending the entire week in our own garage was going to spoil the holiday. 'We'll telephone

Margaret as soon as we can,' I said. All lines were busy the first night so the following morning we were both in the nearest town with a public exchange and spent the entire morning waiting for a free line to London. Finally we spoke to our neighbour.

'Yes, Feckless is all right, she is with me now.' What bliss to hear those words.

It was five a.m., no chance of getting back to sleep so I crept out of bed, I'd decided to make a search once more by a row of garages down a quiet drive. I opened the front door and just couldn't believe my eyes; sitting on the garden fence was a little black cat. 'Feckless,' I called; she jumped off the fence and came quickly towards me. I fumbled at the door in my haste to get back into the house to tell Peter. 'She's here,' I called. 'She's safe.' A very hungry, somewhat dusty Feckless was back with us; she seemed a little disorientated, but nevertheless walked round our legs with her tail in the air. She seemed as pleased to see us as we were overjoyed to see her. I think Feckless might have been shut in some dark place, for she kept blinking as if she hadn't seen daylight for some time. It was only two days, but those two days had seemed a lifetime to us.

CHAPTER 10

HOLIDAY TIME

Tom has one ambition: to gain access to the upper part of the house, Feckless's domain. After breakfast, unless exhausted by night activities, he slips half-way up the stairs to a window-sill. Once there he pretends to be absorbed in anything going on at the front of the house. His aim is for us to forget him so that he can continue his journey upstairs in his search for Feckless. If he meets her on the landing he makes a sound, which I call 'Tom's greeting to Feckless'. It is a cross between the waul he uses with other tom-cats and the tone he uses when in conversation with humans. Feckless in turn will hiss at him before escaping to one of the bedrooms to hide under a bed until rescued by Peter or me. Should Feckless be lying on the bed when Tom enters the room she will jump off to take cover underneath the trailing bed-clothes, sometimes to be joined there by Tom. We usually hear the thud of Feckless jumping off the bed and go upstairs to admonish Tom with calls of 'What a naughty boy!' or, 'Go downstairs, Tom!' He retreats to the dining room, quite unconcerned then jumps into his bed, which is on a chair, and proceeds to knead the soft edges of the cat basket which he has inherited from Feckless. Peter calls this action 'Tom making his bed!' Tom spends a lot of time 'making his bed' before he settles down to snooze away the morning. When Feckless knows the coast is clear, she will come down for her breakfast. Now I think Tom is trying to make friends with Feckless so we decide to put them both into a cattery whilst we take another holiday. Feckless has been there before; she disliked it. Would Tom's presence make her settle? Poorly Puss, who doesn't seek out Feckless was as yet un-neutered and not part of the family.

Whenever we take Feckless anywhere in the car in a cat basket she makes the loudest noise imaginable, making the journey seem twice as long; on this occasion we took the

cats in two cardboard travelling boxes.   What a mistake!
Tom is extremely powerful, in no time he had broken a
corner of his box and almost escaped; I was forced to push
his large head back into the darkness of the box; he pro-
tested loudly, to be joined by Feckless's piteous cry. It was
a nerve-racking journey.   On arrival at the cattery they were
both transferred into plastic coated wire baskets to be carried
to their adjacent quarters.   Feckless immediately retreated
to the sleeping part of the cat run and was not to be seen
again whilst we were there.   Meanwhile, Tom had rushed all
round his outdoor run, back inside to inspect his bed, out
again and he finally managed to trap himself between the
back of his wooden apartment and the wire netting protecting the whole enclosure.   'This won't do,' I said nervously,
'he'll never settle.'

'Yes he will,' the bright voice of the proprietor re-
assured me.   'You leave him to us, don't wait, he'll be quite
all right.'   We left, apprehensive, and crestfallen at Tom's
behaviour.

The week seemed endless; the two cats were constantly
in our minds.   'They can't escape, we know they'll be there
when we return,' Peter said trying to sound cheerful. 'Come
on, enjoy the holiday.'

Once home we set off to the cattery; we took the same
cardboard boxes not wishing to delay our re-union by going
off to buy new cat baskets.   The cardboard boxes had air
holes in them and they were equipped with carrying handles.

Feckless, it appeared, had not left her bed in the inner
compartment of the cat run; she had refused to eat and had
lost weight.   Tom had allowed himself to be handled and
stroked, which he appreciated.   Tom was thought of as a
'fine cat;'   whereas Feckless had alienated herself by
remaining aloof.

We put both the cats in the back of the car having first
transferred them into the cardboard boxes.   We declined an
offer to borrow cat baskets from the cattery, after all we
were going home and it would mean another journey to
return them.   We set off. I sat in the back of the car to talk

36

to the cats and to prevent Tom from getting out. We hadn't proceeded far when, with enormous strength and power Tom thrust his way out of the cat box to freedom in the back of the car; he found his way to the shelf at the rear and demonstrated his nervousness by fouling the area. Feckless had been giving her hideous cry all this time so I decided to let her out to sit on my lap; it might have a calming effect on Tom. Not so, Feckless fought free; now two frightened cats were loose in the car and not remaining still. 'Can't you drive any faster?' I called to Peter, failing to see we were caught up in traffic as I made a grab first for one cat, then the other. 'Got you both!' I held onto the back of their necks until we reached home. Tom was off in a flash to explore the garden; Feckless sulked, demonstrating her disapproval at having been left in a cattery with Tom. At first she refused to eat the dainty morsels of food put out to tempt her appetite. Slowly she came round, then crept down to her food when she thought we weren't looking.

We had not been happy leaving the cats in a cattery although the one we had chosen had been well equipped with heated pads in the beds, and the people running the establishment were kind and understanding, but Feckless's disappointing behaviour made me decide we wouldn't do the same another year. It was far too upsetting. Then I had an idea.

I began to drop hints to my sister about the beauty of the countryside which she and her husband have not seen and which was to be found a short drive from our home. I suggested they came to stay with us using our house as a base for touring, and then I asked her if they would look after the cats to enable us to go away. Much to my surprise she agreed. They are globe trotters; I wasn't sure the countryside of Worcestershire and Warwickshire would hold great appeal to them for they were more accustomed to touring the temples of Asia, or admiring the grandeur of the Himalayas; they have followed in the steps of the Incas and trod the Great Wall of China, but now they were going to explore the countryside close to us, and, they were going to look after the cats.

Feckless made friends with my sister and ate the food

she put before her; she fretted at our absence nevertheless and had a 'lost' air about her. Tom remained aloof but he ate all the food given to him. On our return after a week's absence, Feckless went straight to my sister rubbing herself against my sister's legs; she refused to greet *us*. Once again she demonstrated her disapproval of Peter and me leaving her. Since then we haven't taken a holiday as such, just week-end breaks when our neighbour has cared for the cats. Now, in middle age, Feckless needs more care; daily tablets have to be administered to her. 'I don't think we'll leave Feckless again' I murmur to Peter, 'the boys would be all right, Tom and Poorly Puss, but not Feckless.'

CHAPTER 11

A LAIR IN THE GARDEN

Last night I heard the short, harsh bark of a fox, which is easy to recognize and is quite distinguishable from the bark of a canine, although some people believe foxes are related to the dog. Anyone who has heard the blood-curdling cry of the vixen will not confuse it with any other cry; it never fails to send a shiver down my spine, I begin to worry about the safety of the cats when I hear it. This may be foolish on my part for the foxes are busy with other matters. These urban foxes are multiplying fast and I am not altogether happy about their presence in the towns and cities. They foul the garden, dropping their faeces anywhere on the path or lawn, quite the opposite of the clean cat who will spend a considerable time in covering it's excrement. The foxes raid the dustbins leaving a trail of rubbish behind them; they dig large holes under fences for quick routes of escape; they burrow under sheds and tree stumps leaving earth mounds to spoil the neatness of a well cared for garden. Because of their huge numbers I am concerned in case rabies becomes endemic in this country; it would quickly spread in the towns and I think all pets would have to be destroyed.

Not long ago we discovered a large hole dug under a shed at the bottom of the garden; there was the pungent smell of fox all around. Now it so happened that our local University was doing some research into urban foxes so I contacted the department concerned; they were only too pleased to send researchers along to inspect our garden. It was soon confirmed that we had a fox earth under the shed, probably concealing a vixen; in due course we might see the cubs. The researchers were right, before long three sweet, light tan and cream cubs came out of the earth to play in the garden. They became bold and ventured nearer the house; they also came out in daylight to warm their backs in the sun. The cats were mildly interested, although there was never a confrontation. If the cubs played too close to the house and I noticed one of the cats near them I would go into the garden when my presence would send the young cubs running back to their earth.

We had been told of some well meaning group who caught urban foxes and released them in the country. A couple of it's members looked at the earth in our garden and they were willing to try to catch the cubs; when I discovered they would not attempt to trap the vixen I felt it wasn't fair to separate the young from their mother. Besides, what chance of survival would urban foxes have if released in the country? I had also been informed that since the urban fox has been a scavenger in the towns it has evolved a new jaw-line and no longer hunts as it does in the country; the fox cubs remained safe in our garden. We didn't see them grow to maturity; we just became aware they were no longer with us. The mature foxes had made a well worn path from the rear garden to the front garden, they would jump the fence with a loud clatter to cross the road and vanish into gardens opposite us.

One night when I was calling Feckless in, I noticed a neighbour's cat sitting under a lamp-post opposite me, when suddenly a huge dog fox emerged from the garden behind the cat and strolled by the lamp-post; I held my breath fearful in case the cat moved as I felt sure the fox would pounce, but reynard sauntered unconcernedly across the road.

Contrary to belief, foxes do not spend the daylight hours in their earths only venturing forth at night to forage for food. I have seen a fox sunning itself at noon on the garden shed, and I have also seen a fox strolling round the garden at all times of the day.

When snow is lying on the ground and a full moon lights the garden it is most pleasing to watch the foxes padding around sniffing the ground; a reward indeed for being rudely awakened by the cry of the vixen. In the early hours of one such morning I watched a fox sitting in the snow on its haunches, howling. It was a strange sight. When visitors are staying with us they are often delighted by moonlight glimpses of a fox - a sight they have never seen in the country.

I have seen country foxes for I rode to hounds on my previous mare. I have to admit to having been thrilled by the chase and caught up in the excitement felt by both horse and man. To watch hounds working is a privilege, and yet I am thankful I have never been in at a kill; there have even been one or two occasions when I 'viewed the fox away' but refrained from 'halloaing' his whereabouts. This will dismay true hunting folk and not please the agricultural community; because of these feelings I have quietly dropped out of the scene. I acknowledge that horses are often 'made' in the hunting field; they learn to look after themselves; to take their own line across country thus becoming bolder jumpers; they can also become rejuvenated after a hard season perhaps show jumping or even racing; I know my present mare would benefit from a few runs with the local Hunt, but I lack the motivation, henceforth I shall 'view foxes away' from the seclusion of my garden.

"I have seen country foxes"

CHAPTER 12

FEEDING HABITS

A little black head peeps round the dining-room door whenever Peter and I are eating; it is Feckless looking for the whereabouts of Tom and Poorly Puss before she enters. She has come to find out the menu and plead for any tasty left-overs; a black paw follows as she strives to push the concert-ina door open further to enable her to squeeze in. Peter fitted the door for the sole purpose of keeping the cats out; when we moved in the original dining-room door had been removed to give more light in the passage way and a curtain hung in the entrance. We put the original door back only to find it took up too much space opening into the room. I probably have too much furniture in the dining-room in spite of scaling down before we moved, so it made sense to remove the door.

'Then we had a problem; Feckless became incontinent; she began to use the corners of the dining-room as a litter tray. We cut away pieces of carpet to get rid of the smell. I have yet to find a cleanser that will remove the odour of cat urine, hence the need for the door. We placed another litter tray upstairs, she now had two, but Feckless fouled the bath-room, the toilet and finally a bedroom. More carpet was ripped out and replaced. 'We can't go on like this, Peter,' I said crossly. 'She'll have to go.' Peter knew I didn't mean my threat, but it was embarrassing when visitors called, it became essential to discover the cause of the incontinence. Before we had chance to think of a visit to the veterinary surgery Feckless startled us by behaving very oddly. Early one morning she began to run round in circles then dashed downstairs in a frenzy; she seemed dazed, didn't know where she was. I 'phoned the vet immediately and asked for a house call. The vet called in the afternoon and took Feckless back to the surgery for blood tests. I never cease to admire the efficiency of veterinary surgeons and their practices; they always work quickly and effectively. We were able to collect Feckless by seven o'clock the same evening, the result of the blood tests already known. Little Feckless was suffering from kidney and bladder trouble which was the cause of her incontinence. Modern drugs are marvellous. Feckless now has a long term injection which lasts about ten weeks; since starting the injections she has never once failed to use the litter tray or indicated she would like to go into the garden.

We could think about renewing some of the carpets now Feckless's trouble had been diagnosed. The bathroom and toilet were the first two rooms to receive our attention; soon a warm, scratch-proof carpet replaced the odd hacked about squares which remained in the centre of each room. The dining-room, however, was going to take longer, for Peter had decided to have the chimney-breast removed.

'It will give us more space,' Peter said airily. 'The dining table can go against the back wall, a small table with another television set will fit in nicely where the chimney-breast is.'

We view quite a lot of news programmes; 'All in the interest of work,' Peter says. That's as may be, but sport also flickers across the screen during the week-end; there was an ulterior motive here, I had visions of meals being eaten whilst noisy sports programmes were being televised. We take our meals at odd times for we are often delayed at the stables and it's not unusual to be eating lunch at three o'clock in the afternoon. Still the idea of more space was attractive so I didn't object, then Peter started hinting about the chimney-breast in the bedroom above the dining-room. 'It shouldn't inconvenience us too much,' he said, 'whilst the men are knocking out bricks in the dining-room they might as well do the bedroom.' Before the work started we removed all the dining-room furniture into the lounge; we took the books from my antique dresser and stood them in piles in the sun lounge, the lounge, anywhere we could find a place for them. I didn't know there were so many books on those shelves. The lower part of the dresser we could only convey as far as the hall, there just wasn't room in the lounge with the other large pieces of furniture already there. Antique furniture is a mixed blessing - it takes up an awful amount of space. Most of ours was inherited from my mother, but we happen to like antiques.

Of course, all the bedroom furniture had to be moved out too; we were surrounded by furniture upstairs and downstairs. The cats couldn't understand what was happening, they searched in vain for a favourite armchair, any chair to curl up and hide in.

Then the work started. Oh, the dust, the bricks, the noise. Work went on endlessly, bricks thrown out of the bedroom window to be carted away to a skip; bricks thrown out of the dining-room window - the garden was covered in a film of white dust. I made umpteen pots of tea which were gratefully drunk in the garden by the workmen. The weather was blazing hot.

'We can only work for short periods at a time,' the men said.

'The dust's so thick, will you keep us supplied with tea?' The dust was choking me so I donned a face mask. On one of my many journeys into the garden with tea I forgot to remove it. A neighbour called on me in a flash. 'I can't ask you in there's dust everywhere,' I said as I tried to keep her at the door.

'I haven't come to see your house, I've called to see you.' She was in, peering round the stacked furniture. 'I thought I saw you wearing a mask, are you having to help as well?'

'No! But if you stay long enough you'll need to wear a mask, the dust's unbearable.'

I set to each evening with a broom and a mop, first clearing and then trying to lay the dust.

'I don't know why you bother,' Peter said, 'it'll be just as thick tomorrow.'

Little paw marks made patterns on the floor as the cats investigated the day's work. They were not impressed. Then the men struck a snag. Peter was called in for a conference. I caught snatches of conversation.

'Yes, well obviously you'll have to. How wide will it be?' What did this mean. Peter tried to look unconcerned.

'They've got to fix a support beam, something they'd overlooked. I'm afraid we won't have quite as much space as I'd hoped.'

'You mean we've gone through all this and it isn't going to make much difference?' I could feel my blood pressure rising.

'Now calm down. It means the corner will have a square foot post from floor to ceiling, but we shall still have extra space, just not quite as much. Anyway, the bedroom will be all right.'

'It'll look funny, a square post in the corner of the room.'

'No, they'll box it in and when it's papered you'll hardly notice it.'

I wasn't so sure. But there was nothing to be done. The work seemed to be slowing down. After two weeks they left us for awhile - the cement had to dry.

Was it worth it? Well, if it can be avoided, never have a chimney-breast removed whilst actually living in your house. However, it did create more space in both rooms, that I have to admit is an advantage, and we do have a new carpet.

But back to the cats feeding habits. Feckless knows when I am cooking food she can share with us. The smell of fish being fried or even poached, or a chicken roasted in the oven will bring her into the kitchen where she will sit patiently on the pedal bin. The 'Boys', as we call Tom and Poorly Puss, have not been brought up on home cooking;

they don't wait for the oven door to be opened, although when the carving knife comes out Poorly Puss soon appears.

I feed the cats mostly on tinned cat food and cat biscuits, unless one of them is ill, then I give them freshly cooked fish or chicken. Cheap fish will not do; I soon discovered that Icelandic cod or coley would be left untouched. When we collected Feckless from the veterinary surgery she had to be fed white meat only, as it happened I had none in the house so Peter went to the nearest fish and chip take away to buy fish and cooked chicken, but Feckless was feeling particularly delicate, neither tempted her.

The tinned cat food has to be of the best quality too, the cheaper brands are wasted for after tasting the first mouthful the food is left uneaten, and it's no use leaving it in the vain hope it will be eaten when they're hungry, they would rather starve. Each cat has it's own feed bowl; Tom and Poorly Puss are fed in the kitchen, Feckless has her food on a tray in the hall. Tom may not understand the smell of a chicken being roasted but he can certainly smell the bones in the pedal bin. If he thinks he is not observed he will gingerly lift the lid of the bin with his head before thrusting a paw inside to retrieve a leg or wing. He is quite clever at this and manages to reach a long way down to recover a piece of the carcase however well wrapped up. I don't encourage this, nevertheless it demonstrates his background and I think it proves that he kept himself alive by scavenging. I very occasionally cook 'lights' for the 'Boys'; Feckless's palate is far too superior to touch meat of that order, she will shake a paw if that sort of food is put in front of her, before walking off in disgust. I find I have to open three tins of cat food each day, for they eat at least two and a half large tins; the 'Boys' are fed by others too, for they like to keep in with my close neighbours who know at once when we are away from the house by the presence of the cats.

I've recently read about an automatic feeding device for cats, I'm wondering whether to treat Feckless to one. It's a covered feed bowl which opens it's lid by pre-set timing thus preventing the food from drying out. An ice pack can be placed beneath the food to keep it cool in summer. Perhaps that would be pampering her too much since we seldom leave her alone all day.

46

Poorly Puss's day begins at seven o'clock when he has his first breakfast at a neighbour's house across the road. He then queues up for milk at the French window of another neighbour and by the time we open our back door he is waiting with Tom to enter the house for his second breakfast. Tom comes in first, for as I've already mentioned, the rear of the house is his territory; Poorly Puss being aware of this, hangs back a couple of paces.

When we enter the house by the front door Tom, who has got bolder since we adopted him will often sneak in behind Poorly Puss. Feckless is usually inside; these days she spends more time indoors either keeping warm by a radiator if it's winter, or sitting in a sunny spot on an upstairs window-sill. When she goes out she waits until the 'Boys' are both in the house then goes to the lounge door to indicate her wish to be let out, which means opening the door into the sun lounge and letting her out into the garden through that room. She comes back the same way; this can prove a nuisance for in wet weather all manner of twigs or leaves are brought in and her muddy paws leave foot marks on clean floors or carpets. Occasionally in the summer she ventures round to the back door to make her entrance if she thinks Tom and Poorly Puss are inside and the coast is clear.

Poorly Puss has put on so much weight he now weighs 11 lbs. He spends much of the day sitting by his empty feed bowl in the vain hope it will be replenished. I have threatened to put him on a diet, but it would only mean he would visit the neighbours more often. He can no longer jump the fence with ease; Peter on observing his difficulty decided to erect a plank between a large wisteria tree and the fence dividing a neighbour's garden. Now all the cats make use of this walk-way and I doubt if Poorly Puss could get down without it. I believe cats are not susceptible to arthritis unless they have suffered an injury, nor do they die from a heart condition, so I am not unduly worried by his weight. Nevertheless I have decided to change his name; it may once have been appropriate to call him Poorly Puss but he is far from poorly now. I am trying out Porgy, it sounds similar to Poorly; on the other hand I should like to call him Rumpole. Rumpole of the Old Bailey is being shown on television and Poorly is a big, soft, cuddly pussy-cat who reminds me of Rumpole. Even when he was neutered the vet couldn't bring himself to write Poorly Puss on his card, instead he wrote 'stray male' and left his name a blank. Rumpole it shall be, for my maiden name is Bailey.

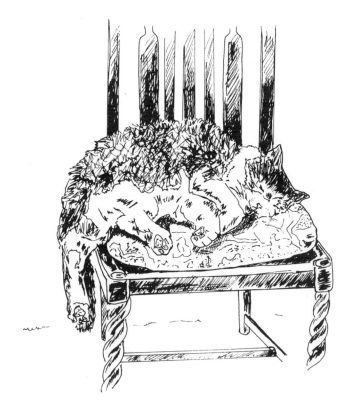

"Rumpole"

CHAPTER 13

CAT AT SEA

Peter spent the Second World War in the Merchant Navy. Of the number of cats he encountered whilst at sea one remains fresh in his mind; he was serving on the R.M.S. "Marquessa" when one of the crew brought a young, black cat aboard when the ship had docked at Liverpool. He had brought it to join the ship's company ostensibly to keep down the rat population.

The ship's doctor was an elderly Welshman, a native of Caerphilly, and as might be expected he was for ever praising it's cheese. The doctor's career before taking to the sea was chequered to say the least. He was a jovial character, huge-framed and plumpish; he was also fond of his drink and a great raconteur of somewhat doubtful stories. Now the doctor had two pet aversions; ships' stokers and Germans, the latter one could understand for he had been wounded in the First World War which had left him with a permanent limp. Why he objected to stokers was a little more obscure.

One lunch time when the ship had berthed at Monti-video to discharge cargo, a seaman came bursting into the saloon to announce that the young cat had fallen into one of the ship's holds and appeared to be badly hurt. Instantly the elderly doctor was on his feet hurrying out on deck to see what assistance he could give. Peter went ashore that after-noon; returning to the ship later in the day he enquired the fate of the cat. The helpless animal couldn't walk; the doctor, who had found compassion for the young feline, had taken it to his cabin where he had made a bed for it and declared 'they should not be disturbed.'

The cat received the doctor's constant attention, and so good were his administrations that after about a week the doctor brought the young cat out on deck. It moved about very slowly and this exercise was only allowed under the strict supervision of the doctor. The young animal gradually improved and even started to play, but it was obvious some damage had occurred to the tail which always remained limp as the tail was dragged along behind the cat. This didn't appear to worry the animal in any way for within a month he was as lively and playful as ever. The doctor was thought of more highly after demonstrating his skill and devotion in helping the cat towards recovery. But, his attitude to ships' stokers and Germans remained unchanged. Did it need a ships' stoker to fall down one of the holds to bring about a change of heart? We shall never know.

CHAPTER 14

THE HUNTERS

Feckless is a very inquisitive cat; she is much more inquisitive than Tom or Poorly Puss; she is always keen to know where we have been and keen to investigate any parcels that have been brought home. Anything new has to be inspected; if we have been out in the car the whole vehicle is given a thorough examination, paying particular attention to the tyres by sniffing all four. Perhaps the tyres pick up tell tale smells of our journey which conveys much to her; no doubt she can smell the stable cats when we return from the farm. After a careful examination she sits on the bonnet, occasionally she looks inside if a door has been left open, but the inside of cars does not appeal to Feckless.

This inquisitiveness prompted Feckless to inspect the inside of my next-door-neighbour's house; a neighbour I don't know very well, but who has informed me that she is allergic to cats. One day, Feckless surprised this neighbour, who was bathing her young son, by suddenly appearing in the bathroom; she peeped over the rim of the bath to inspect the young boy in the water; squeals of laughter from the three year old sent Feckless scurrying home. Bathrooms hold a fascination for Feckless; she is always trying to get into the airing cupboard to hide amongst the clothes, this I can understand, but when she is denied entry she hits out at the light cord in temper whereupon the swinging cord in turn hits the bathroom mirror. I know she inspects the empty bath for I've often noticed her paw marks round the rim and on the bottom of the bath, even in the wash hand basin. She can't be searching for a drink of water, for water is always left for the cats in the kitchen.

Feckless also takes a keen interest in anything she finds in the garden; she chases butterflies, makes hopeless attempts to catch flies, even wasps or bees; all insects keep her constantly amused.   One warm day I found her playing with a young frog.   This was something she hadn't encountered before, she found the frog most intriguing;   I rescued the frog countless times placing him in a clump of St. John's Wort, but Feckless discovered his hiding place or else he hopped out not wishing to be hidden there;   in the end I took Feckless into the house and found a shady spot among some damp ferns to deposit the frog.   I hope he survived.

I have never seen Feckless catch a bird - the only birds she is interested in are table birds.   If I have placed a freshly cooked fowl on the kitchen work-top having failed to close the kitchen door, Feckless has been known to slip in unobserved and jump onto the work surface to steal a meal. A faint tinkle of the plate being knocked about gives the game away.   I am most displeased with the little thief, who is quite unrepentant.

Tom, on the other hand, stalks small birds and will bring one to the back door for my inspection;   it is difficult to be cross with him for he is only satisfying his natural instinct; I assume he has killed the bird - the bird is always dead when presented to me.

I do not take kindly to mice and did not realize Feckless's prowess in hunting mice until I spied her from a bedroom window crossing the road with something in her mouth;   I raced downstairs to find out what she had caught and if whatever it was still lived;   I had intended to keep Feckless outside but she eluded me and ran upstairs with her prize;   I followed her into a bedroom to discover she held a tiny field mouse in her mouth which was very much alive. What followed can only be called a pantomime, a pantomime I do not wish to repeat.   First Feckless released the mouse only to pounce on it again, rushing round to avoid being caught by me;   when I did catch Feckless and made her release the mouse, the mouse escaped only to disappear in some obscure corner.   I shut Feckless out of the room, waited awhile to let the mouse settle, returned to the room with a plastic carrier bag which I hoped to pop the mouse into, but then I lost the mouse altogether;   I had to bring Feckless back to flush out the mouse from it's hiding place. This scene was re-enacted several times before I managed to trap the little field mouse in the carrier bag, whereupon I dashed outside and promptly released it in overgrown grass on a path leading to some tennis courts. I returned to a disgruntled Feckless who had to be kept in the house until she had forgotten all about the mouse.

Poorly Puss is not a hunter. He always relies on his good looks, his expressive eyes and appealing behaviour to break down any resistance on the part of humans who might wish to refrain from feeding him. As a last resort he rolls over to reveal the soft, snow white fur of his tummy; this never fails to bring forth words of praise followed, naturally, by food and drink.

"Feckless released the mouse only to pounce on it again"

CHAPTER 15

THE HUBBUB

Peter and I were drinking a mid-morning cup of coffee in the garden. The sun was warm. There was no sign of the cats. No doubt they were having a cat-nap in a shaded part of the garden, although usually one of them appeared if they sensed we were about. Soon the quiet of the garden was shattered by the loudest chattering and bird squawking I have ever heard. Numerous birds were flitting backwards and forwards from one tree to another at the bottom of the garden. We both jumped up and raced down the garden fearing one of the cats had caught a bird. Many birds, both small and large were dive-bombing in and out of one of the tall cypresses. Looking upwards we discovered the reason. A large tawny owl was perched in a fork of the tree, blinking his eyes as the birds darted about. The sun shone on him and revealed all his splendour. It was a fantastic sight. The whole bird population of the garden appeared to have ganged up in an attempt to drive the owl away. Peter fetched his binoculars; we studied the owl's colouring and observed the shading in his feathers, his flattened facial disk and black eyes. We stood gazing up into the tree mugs of coffee in our hands. He was in no hurry to depart. A jumbo-jet roared away overhead having taken off from our local airport some ten miles away. The owl's big neck swivelled round as he followed the sound. The bird activity ceased momentarily. Peter and I left the scene to set about our various tasks. Checking on him at lunchtime we found he was in the same position. Another visit in the early afternoon found him sitting motionless, eyes closed. Later still, when the shadows had lengthened, he was still there. The birds had ceased their chattering long ago. All was quiet. Earlier I had spotted a tiny wren joining in the fracas with the other birds. What a brave little fellow! The resident robin had been prominent, a couple of blackbirds had squawked their alarm call, and I had seen a noisey magpie hopping through the branches.   Blue tits had darted in and out of the tree and house sparrows had added to the general hubbub.

'Do you think the owl had just flown into the tree?' I asked Peter.

'Well, we were sitting in the garden before all the noise started.   We thought the cats were up to mischief.   I really don't know.'

It was odd that not one of the cats had appeared.   With so much activity going on I expected at least one cat's curiosity to have got the better of it.

A few hours passed.   We made a visit to the stables; not wishing to spend too much time there, we walked through the fields to examine Millie to ensure all was well with her, deciding not to ride.   On our return we hurried eagerly into the garden.   The tree was empty.   Occasionally an owl hoots at night.   I like the sound.   Is it the same owl re-visiting our garden?

I had always believed that owls did not emerge before dusk to hunt their prey; until I encountered the little owl at Alcott Farm.   An old oak tree stands in one of the fields flanking the drive-way to the house.   Using this tree as it's base the little owl ventures forth in broad daylight.   Sometimes it will perch on a telegraph post and waggle it's head if it becomes suspicious.   We have disturbed it many times upon entering the drive from the narrow road.   If any attempt is made to get a closer look by stopping the car to focus binoculars on the owl it is away in a flash.

I have never had any success in getting close to it when on horseback.   I once set off down the drive at a steady pace whilst viewing the owl on a distant post.   As I advanced I thought I was going to be lucky.   The owl knew better.   It rose from the post with a quick movement and turning it's undulating body flew to the oak tree, where only it's outline was visible.   I have not seen it make a kill, although I understand that the little owl will tackle a bird as big as itself.

My other encounter with an owl when on horseback goes back quite a few years to the time when barn owls were more common. One winter's evening I was taking part in a group riding lesson in an indoor school at a large riding establishment. Six or seven of us were riding our horses through various exercises when suddenly there was a flutter above our heads and what appeared to be a large white bird flew up into the rafters. When the excited horses had settled down and we all felt a little calmer, the white apparition turned out to be a barn owl. Viewed from below it was obvious it was not all white. The barn owl was keen to get out to it's hunting ground. It made several attempts to find an exit, each time returning to it's perch in the rafters. The instructor taking the class decided to open the huge school doors and to turn out the electric lights. It was quite dark outside and even darker inside the school. To keep the horses occupied we rode them quietly in a single file inside the building, each of us staying close to the horse in front. Horses are creatures of habit, so following a well-trodden track - something they have done hundreds of times - is not as strange as it may sound. Like cats, horses also have a certain amount of night vision. In addition, they have acute hearing. Also like cats, their face whiskers act as feelers.

It was quite eerie riding in the dark. We were told to whistle to make us relax. A nervous rider can transmit tension to an animal. It would not do to get the horses upset, any playing about such as a horse kicking out, rearing up or taking a bite at another animal could cause a lot of trouble.

After a time - it seemed an eternity - the lights were switched on. Someone giggled nervously as we grew accustomed to the lights. Looking upwards our eyes searched the rafters. They were empty. The barn owl had silently flown away.

"The owl knew better"

CHAPTER 16

OTHER CATS

Anyone who keeps a cat will know it's no surprise to find interesting feline characters among one's friends' cats. More often than not the said animal has invited it's way into the household to become one of the family. The female cat of an ex-colleague of mine likes to eat cocktail biscuits; Topsy will stand on her hind legs begging a biscuit from her mistress or anyone whose attention she can gain. It is a party piece which warrants praise and promotes conversation, if only to say 'what a clever girl!' or 'What a beautiful, clever girl.'

Kippur, so named because he first appeared on Yom Kippur, the Jewish Day of Atonement, proves to be a boxer. In true fighting spirit he spars behind a plate glass door; his opponent, a big tabby from across the road. They stand on hind legs throwing blows to each other in mock battle as they prance up and down the length of the sliding door, each one aware that it's safe behind the glass. This comic sight has amused dinner party guests on many occasions; guests have watched fascinated to see which cat will tire first; sometimes it will be the tabby, sometimes Kippur; after a brief pause the next round is resumed; the game continues as paw matches paw sliding along the glass; quite suddenly Kippur declares himself the winner; he has grown tired of boxing, the tabby might as well go home.

I believe Poorly Puss fathered Jasper and Jemima, the two cats belonging to neighbours across the road. He certainly takes a fatherly interest in both. Occasionally he will admonish one with a cuff on the ear, but for the most part they are reasonably well tolerated, any other cat would receive a hearty swipe from Poorly Puss or be chased away.

Peter has often told me tales of his years spent in New

Zealand, but I hadn't heard about the marmalade cat which his sister, Valerie, adopted until I began to write this story. It was during the time of the great earthquake in Napier on the north island of New Zealand in 1931, when the earthquake forced the land to rise many feet resulting in land slides which totally demolished many houses forcing the families to be evacuated. The short-haired marmalade cat had been found wandering about in a state of severe shock when it was rescued by people leaving the area. They brought the cat to Peter's family and Valerie took it under her wing. She had a harness fitted to the scared animal for it was necessary to keep it on a lead until the state of shock passed. It was a beautiful cat which Valerie called Tigger after one of the characters in A.A. Milne's book "The House at Pooh Corner" which she was reading at the time. It was the custom for most houses in New Zealand to have fire escapes attached to them, probably because so many houses were built entirely of wood, but unlike the sturdy fire escapes on houses in this country, the one on Peter's house was merely an extended ladder attached to the wall. It had a gap at the bottom to prevent intruders from climbing on to it. Members of the household were able to release the missing part from the top of the ladder. It was Tigger's habit to run up the fire escape, jump through the window to land on Peter's bed below, giving him a momentary fright if he happened to be still in bed. Sadly, Tigger had to be given to friends when the family came to England.

Thoughts of other cats known to me come flooding in; my brother's kitten who likes to climb the open staircase in his house in order to pounce on any unsuspecting person beneath; a cat who travels everywhere with my niece and has thus become as much at home in other people's houses as his own; a friend who moved house and lost her cat just as they were departing only to see him emerge from a packing case in their new home. The list is endless.

How is it when cats adopt us they know we are going to look after them? They never fail to find a loving home when they arrive looking forlorn and neglected on someone's doorstep. Has nature endowed them with psychic powers? If such powers exist.

CHAPTER 17

VETERINARY SURGERIES

Feckless is due for her ten weekly booster drug so I pad the travelling cat basket with newspaper; I know we won't be kept waiting long at the surgery, the paper is a precaution against the stress of travelling in the car which Feckless dislikes. Once there she settles down to watch the activity of cats and dogs coming and going. There is a friendly atmosphere; animals break the ice anywhere, people talk to each other, admire the waiting cats in their different baskets and enquire the reason for their visit. Unlike a doctor's waiting room, or worse still, a dentist's waiting room where one is greeted by an icy atmosphere and deathly silence, only the name of the next patient being called breaking that silence, no-one enquires if you are waiting for an extraction or a filling, or is it just a routine check? Periodicals are glanced through without really absorbing one's interest. Back at the waiting room of the veterinary surgery soothing words are spoken to sick animals; whimpering dogs are coaxed into silence. Some cats are held in blankets, others come attached to a harness. The merits of the different travelling baskets on the market are discussed; in no time one's name is called and you take your pet into the inner sanctum of one of the examination rooms. When Feckless is taken out of her basket she starts to purr under the caring hands of the veterinary surgeon. I have often remarked on this for in no way does she show distress or fear at being placed on a table in a strange place. No doubt she relishes the attention. Nor does she object when the needle is pushed in; after a careful examination we are on our way home.

Last summer I noticed a small lump on Poorly Puss's right ear; I promptly made an appointment for him with my kind vet. Poorly Puss was hospitalized and the lump removed; it was a small cancerous growth. Part of the recovery treatment was to keep him out of the sunshine; this

60

proved difficult for on warm, sunny days he loves to lie in the sun. His right ear is white and therefore more sensitive to light and sunshine; he made a complete recovery.

Poorly Puss doesn't have a voice. He opens his mouth, tries to talk but no sound comes forth. Even when transporting him to the surgery he is silent, his mouth opens and closes in vain. The vet believes he may have had cat influenza when a kitten which might have affected his vocal chords. Before we had Poorly Puss neutered Feckless was receiving hormone tablets which made her interesting to male cats; then Poorly Puss broke his silence - he startled us by caterwauling loudly. Deciding he should be Feckless's guardian he never left her side; he sat next to her under the car, he followed her across the road into other gardens; he dogged her footsteps; he sat quietly next to her on a garden wall and he never let her out of his sight. Understandably Feckless objected to so much attention; her life was becoming a nightmare; reluctantly we decided to take her off the hormone tablets, which were to promote growth of hair which she was losing. She was put on a daily thyroid tablet instead, and these she still receives.

Tom is the youngest of our three charges, although his exact age is not known; the vet thought he was about two years old when we had him neutered. His only return visit to the surgery was when he recently developed an inflamed throat.

I have been very fortunate with my veterinary surgeons. I have complete faith in all of them. I say all of them because the small animals' veterinary surgery does not prescribe for large animals, so my Thoroughbred mare, Millie, is under another group of veterinary surgeons. The mare was bred by a vet who runs a practice within visiting distance of the stables where Millie is at livery. What could be nicer than having her breeder keep an eye on one of the fine animals he has bred? She came to us with the registered name of Most Indignant; and she was so named because of her most indignant behaviour. How well it suits her; she puts on a most indignant look in the stable if things are not to her liking. For instance, when she is brought to the stable from the fields if the hay rack is empty, she will swing round to face the door, give a haughty look, swing round to the empty rack then back to her handler whom she proceeds to push in the ribs as if to say 'This isn't good enough, where's my hay!' We enter her as Most Indignant for all competitions we take part in, but Most Indignant is too much of a mouthful to say in the stable, or call in the fields. We spent many happy hours thinking of and trying out different names, such as: Honey, Tango, Emma, Minty until finally we settled for Millie. The name Millie rolls off the tongue easily; it also carries well across the fields when equal emphasis can be given to both syllables - Mill Lee.

Sometimes I call at the large animals' surgery to collect medication or worming paste. On one such trip to the town surgery of my horse vet I was amazed to see two heifers loaded in a horse trailer in the car park. They had been brought in for urgent injections - just a routine job for the vet.

A road sweeper with flashing lights has just passed along the road outside our house; I heard Feckless jump off the bed in the room above me, now she has done her disappearing act, we cannot find her anywhere, so clever is she at melting into the surroundings. Tom and Poorly Puss are quite unconcerned, sleeping on their respective chairs. Different sounds upset them; the doorbell or the telephone ringing are both noises alien to the 'Boys'; they take flight immediately rushing to the nearest door to get outside. Whereas Feckless is curious, she will appear from nowhere to investigate the visitor at the door, or to take part in the telephone conversation. Peter has called out he has found her! She was hiding beneath a long velvet curtain in another bedroom. Usually she feels safe hiding underneath the bed, not this time.

If I had met the road sweeper whilst riding Millie she would have been very scared of the flashing lights; her first reaction would have been to run away from the horrid vehicle; having found she couldn't as I would have been restraining her she would prance on the spot whilst snorting to indicate her nervousness. Usually it is small things which terrify her; on windy days she will see ghosts in every corner; if the sun shines she will find her shadow baffling enough to take fright and spook all the way back to the stables.

Some veterinary surgeries for large animals have well equipped modern operating theatres; if a horse has to be given an anaesthetic the danger, as well as from the anaesthetic, is in the horse falling heavily and possibly injuring itself. One method, after tranquilising the animal, is to use an operating table which can be moved into a vertical position to enable the animal to be led up alongside the table and strapped to it; as the anaesthetic begins to take effect and the muscles relax, the table is swung into a horizontal position thus allowing the animal to lie on it. An anaesthetist is always in attendance as well as the veterinary surgeon carrying out the operation.

Surgeries without this operating table have the floor and walls of the operating room heavily padded, and to assist the animal to go down gently, new drugs have been developed which allow the horse to fall almost on a pre-determined spot with little more force than that produced by the horse lying down normally.

My previous mare was taken to a modern surgery for an exploratory operation in a vain hope to diagnose her illness and hopefully to find a cure for her. She had lost condition quickly and was in some distress with her breathing. I think in my heart I knew she was fading, but I had to explore every avenue open to me in an attempt to find the cause of her illness. It would have been kinder to have had her humanely destroyed on home ground; in surroundings she knew and therefore would not be frightened nor suspicious. But, there was a faint hope, just a glimmer that the vet might be able to perform a miracle. I had to take a chance; reluctantly I let her go. In the end it proved unsuccessful - how I regretted allowing the mare to spend her last days in strange surroundings, away from friends, both equine and human. I shed painful tears when I gave permission for her days to be ended. Dear Donna, she was seventeen years old, not old for a horse, some live to twenty-five or thirty. Even now tears fill my eyes when I think of Donna; I shall never again feel as much for a horse as I did for that kind mare. Or am I steeling myself against such an attachment towards Millie?

The veterinary surgeon was sympathetic; he had done all in his power to save her. When he carried out a post mortem he discovered she had a very large aneurism in the gut, about the size of a clenched fist. In addition there were several nodules in her upper nostrils. There would have been no hope on both counts.

Veterinary surgeons have my respect and admiration. They perform Herculean tasks, not all as unfruitful as my experience with Donna, most are rewarding; their silent patients are unable to thank them - I salute them with all my heart.

CHAPTER 18

INDIFFERENT CATS

'Look out Tom!' I called too late, with a loud thud Tom was on the floor having fallen out of his bed; it was placed as usual on a chair, but Tom had been lying to the front of his bed, the effort of shifting his weight had made him roll out. Surprisingly, Poorly Puss in the next instance had joined him on the floor having rolled off the chair he had been lying on, his huge frame had been draped over the side of the chair, with his hind legs dangling down. He had not looked comfortable, but he chose to lie there having steadfastly refused to go to his bed. Whenever we notice one of the 'Boys' curled up in a precarious position we place a dining room chair in front of the bed; thus temporarily imprisoned the cat peers out from behind bars. Never before have they both fallen to the ground at the same time.

When asleep Tom grooms one ear, washing the same spot continuously; then he hides his face, covering his eyes with a white paw; he moves his position to tuck his head down, loud sonorous vibrations come from his cat bed - he is snoring.

Poorly Puss, on the other hand, goes all soft and silly before he goes to sleep, having climbed onto one of our laps he purrs loudly whilst putting his tongue out, then little droplets of saliva fall from his mouth. But, his first priority is food; the sound of a meal being prepared in the kitchen makes him jump off his comfortable temporary bed to hasten to his feed bowl; he is very greedy. When nothing is forthcoming he returns to seek out the warm lap he had earlier relinquished; as he jumps up waving his bushy tail Tom invariably thrusts out a paw in an attempt to grab the tail; it is an immediate reflex action for Tom appears to be asleep; awake in an instant he now sits up blinking his

eyes. 'No, it's not time to move Tom, go back to sleep.'
He turns around two or three times then settles down.

'What are you doing?' Peter asked me, poking his
head round the bedroom door.
'I'm about to practise some Yoga exercises, but first
I'm trying to 'slip a second'. Close the door I don't want
to be disturbed.' This last remark, as Peter knew, was meant
to keep Feckless out. However, in no time after he had
departed, I heard a loud thud against the door as Feckless
pushed with all the strength of her little body to open the
door. I was lying on the floor so she clambered on my chest.
'Feckless, how can I practise Yoga with you sitting there?'
I addressed her little face as she sat peering at me; in spite of
her small frame she is quite heavy. 'Ah, well, perhaps I'll
just try to relax.' She tentatively reached out a paw to
touch my cheek. This meant stroke me please. I brought
a hand up and stroked her under the chin. Every time I
stopped she pushed her head down asking for more, purring
softly, quite content to remain there. 'Well, I've got work
to do Feckless, you'll have to move.' It was no good
attempting to relax. Feckless didn't heed me, so I struggled
into a sitting position and she very awkwardly walked down
one of my legs. She likes to sit close to one of us. When we
are in bed she will position herself on a pillow, periodically
putting out a paw to attract attention. If I cover my head
with a sheet she will pull at the cover as if to say 'This won't
do you haven't stroked me.' It is necessary to close one's
eyes when Feckless is in this mood for she usually purrs
whilst at the same time opening and closing her claws whilst
she stretches out a paw.

Poorly Puss makes the loudest noise when purring - it
sounds like an engine. Tom's purr is more restrained. Tom
doesn't like being handled, he feels very vulnerable if anyone
tries to pick him up.

Feckless, also, refuses to be picked up. Whenever it is
necessary to spray the cats with an anti-flea powder Feckless
manages to hide, sensing what we are about, when we do
catch her she protests loudly whilst the spraying is taking
place. It is practically impossible to do Tom satisfactorily,
he struggles too fiercely, scratching the arms of whoever's

66

holding him.   There is no time to brush his coat in the opposite direction;   speed in carrying out the operation is essential.   Poorly Puss likes nothing better than to feel a brush or comb on his back or be gathered up in one's arms, but he does not remain too still when the noise of the spray is heard.

Feckless is very independent, only seeking us out if she so wishes.   She will jump on a lap if it suits her, we cannot pick her up and put her there.   She can also be very indifferent.   When I came home after my spell in the hospital, all eager to see the cats, Feckless completely ignored me.   She gave no sign of pleasure at my return, no rubbing against my legs, no sound of purring.   I felt quite rejected.   Peter had taken care of her, she had no need for me and for a day or so she remained aloof.   Poorly Puss gave me quite a generous welcome, but that was partly self interest, trying to entice me to feed him.   Nothing from Tom in the way of a greeting. It was most disappointing, I am sure they had not missed me. I decided to give them a talking to.   'Listen to me boys and girl.   I want a little attention, please, furthermore' I tell them, 'I am thinking of immortalising you, so watch out, I want a show of affection or I might change my mind!'

"Listen to me boys and girl, I want a little attention"

67

CHAPTER 19

THE BLACKSMITH

Monday is the day the blacksmith calls at the stables; he parks his van containing the mobile forge then walks round the stables examining each horse in turn until John or a groom appears to give him the day's requirements.

'Five full sets to-day, Bert. The new grey, Dandy Buck, Fitz, Will and Cecil. Road studs for Phyllis.' Bert nods his head. I hurry over to him.

'If I bring Millie out will you rasp a risen clench for me Bert?'

'Yes, I'll do her right away.' I lead my horse over to the blacksmith and he taps the hoof with his rasp to make the clench rise even more then he cuts it off flush to the wall of the hoof with his pincers and finishes with a final rasp to make sure it is smooth. The clenches or nails sometime rise if the ground is hard, or if too much fast work is done on the road; if the risen clench is on the inside of the shoe it can cause injury to the other foot so it is necessary to have them all smooth. Seven clenches is the usual number used to keep a shoe firmly fixed to a horse's hoof.

The blacksmith lost his wife just before Christmas; through an unfortunate misunderstanding word got round that it was Bert who had died, not his wife. Several letters of condolence were dispatched before the error was discovered. People began ringing up other farriers in their haste to find another blacksmith, for good blacksmiths are worth their weight in gold; their working days so long it is not easy to fit in new customers. Bert is a changed man; he looks greyer, is quieter; formerly I was able to share a joke with him, now I feel embarrassed, not wishing to joke I chatter away about unimportant things; I know he is not listening, he gathers up his tool box takes hold of a horse's front leg and begins to remove a shoe. Calor gas cylinders heat coke into which cold steel shoes are placed; soon the sound of a hammer striking the anvil rings out as he shapes the red hot shoes to the right size; Bert refashions ready made shoes; the pungent smell of burning hoof fills the air as he fits the shoe to the horse's foot. Heidi nips through the open stable door to take away pieces of hoof which have been trimmed. There cannot be many jobs as back-aching as a blacksmith's, bending low holding a horse's leg between his own legs. Bert wears a huge leather apron tied round his waist; it gives him some protection should a horse kick out when he is holding a red hot shoe in his hand. Occasionally a horse will be startled and pull away suddenly, knocking over the tool box and scattering the nails; a sharp reprimand will be given then he is back to calming the frightened animal. Bert is kind, but firm, he stands no nonsense; the unhurried work continues. We are lucky, he visits our stable yard once a week; my mare gets a new set of shoes every four to six weeks according to how much road work we have done.

When I lived in Hest Bank in those far off days I had to hack my pony to the next village to have him shod. I kept two of Snowball's shoes as a reminder of his tiny, neat feet; the collection has grown, two large front shoes from Donna rest beside the original pair dwarfing them even more; these have been joined by two of Millie's small shoes. Horse shoes are supposed to bring good luck, like black cats; my little black cat disgraced herself yesterday.

I took some friends home for tea, having prepared smoked salmon rolls; now whenever we have visitors Feckless has to satisfy her curiosity by inspecting the newcomers. Will they make a fuss of her? Has she met them before? She walks round each individual sniffing round ankles and legs, even shoes are examined; if someone appeals to her she jumps on their lap - not mine or Peter's, it has to be one of the visitors; she was not particularly welcomed this time for we were having tea sitting in the lounge with plates balanced on our laps, cups of tea were on low tables; Feckless's keen sense of smell soon located the smoked salmon rolls, she wrinkled her nose in anticipation, I quickly removed the plate from the lower shelf of the trolley; Feckless was in a reckless mood, she decided to examine the next offering, a plate of egg and cress rolls, these were soon dismissed; finally she jumped onto a low table and with an angry movement gave the chocolate gateau a striking blow with her paw.   By this time I was holding an armful of plates and could not rescue the cake.   'Feckless, you naughty girl.   Get down at once!' I addressed her in my cross voice. She slowly moved off the table and without a backward glance haughtily left the room.

Feckless's curiosity extends to night prowling; visitors staying overnight are advised to firmly close the bedroom door for Feckless on the prowl in the early hours is known to thrust her weight against a door to gain admittance. Once in it is a short jump from the floor to the bed and a sleeping visitor often gets a rude awakening.   After inspection of the prone person she may decide to settle by the pillow, but more often she settles half-way down the bed.   There is not a great deal of room in a single bed for both Feckless and the occupant; if they succeed in pushing her off the bed she will curl up quite happily on a bedroom chair.   Visits to the bathroom can also be hazardous for a black shape will often emerge to brush against one's legs; confining her to our bedroom results in either piteous mewing or hearty scratching of the door. I suppose we spoil her as we leave food downstairs in her usual feeding place for these nightly prowls; should insufficient be left out we are soon informed by little feet stamping on the pillow all around our heads, or constant jumping on and off the bed until one of us reluctantly goes downstairs to replenish the empty dish.   The 'Boys' too are given food to ward off night starvation; we have a nightly ritual, Poorly Puss's dish is taken to the garage by Peter followed by me carrying the huge fellow in my arms.   He loves being carried. We go through the lounge into the sun lounge and thence the garage.   Poorly Puss becomes limp in my arms - a characteristic of the Ragdoll cat breed - he hangs loosely over my arms like a ragdoll.   During the winter months we run a tubular heater to warm the garage, which Poorly Puss can leave by way of a cat flap if he wishes. Tom also has a heater in the boiler house for the colder nights, it lies beneath his bed so he is really snug.   It did not take Poorly Puss long to learn how to use the cat flap - my chief concern at present is that he will get too big to operate it, or get stuck half-way through and have to be rescued by the fire brigade! He is too big to enter Tom's house, which is a good thing as a little sparring takes place when they queue up to be the first across the threshold. If Poorly Puss gets in first he hides behind the opened door ready to attack Tom, but Tom is becoming braver he has started to position himself in the most strategic place for first entry. Poorly Puss loses any advantage he might have had by rushing to greet us. These days Feckless will only venture outside if she knows the 'Boys' are both in the house, or at least that Tom is, for he tends to chase her. Should Tom be in the garden when Feckless wishes to venture out we go in search of him.

'It's all right, he's gone over the fence. All clear, Feckless.' One of us calls. Very hesitantly she walks the few yards from the sun lounge door to the flower beds; sometimes Tom will sense she is out and return to taunt her; how I wish she would hold her ground, but she rushes back to hide beneath a chair. In warmer weather she stays under a garden chair if we are sitting out too. In her younger days we had games in the garden with a flightless golf ball; happy hours were spent practising golf shots which would send her scampering all over the garden. These games took place inside as well for Feckless was just as happy to play with a toffee paper as with a golf ball. Nowadays games are played in the bedroom or along the corridor; mad scampers as if she has seen a ghost; chasing her tail whilst on a bed; delving under a counterpane; grabbing a hand to bite and worry, games with a piece of string ending up with a race along the corridor to enter the room in which she sharpens her claws. The years fall away from her - she is a kitten once more.

When I consider the different eating habits of our three cats it strikes me that females are daintier eaters than tom-cats or neutered toms. Feckless settles down to a meal with her tail curled neatly round her body and delicately picks up tasty morsels in small bites, eating slowly. When the 'Boys' eat neither of them curls his tail round his body, the tails remain straight; Tom's short unattractive tail appears stiff; whereas Poorly Puss's tail, because it is thick, bushy and long at least appears to have some life in it, even though it is held out straight. Both drop food as they eat; Tom is in a great

71

hurry, he gobbles his meal as if he isn't sure where or when the next meal will come from; the big fellow takes more time, savouring each mouthful until his bowl is empty, then he sits quietly waiting for more. They both drink milk in a very sloppy manner spilling half the contents of a saucer on to the floor. I think they try to drink too quickly. Poorly Puss comes away with wet whiskers and milk covering his lower jaw; Tom at least wipes his face clean and the Queen Bee has no need to conceal the fact she has been eating, not a trace of food or milk is to be seen on her face or round her mouth, so dainty is her action.

CHAPTER 20

A CHANGE OF PLANS

Peter has made a decision. 'We're taking a holiday,' he told me this morning. 'You need a break in the sun. I'll get hold of some brochures.'

He was off before I had time to argue the point. Well, it wasn't final, he had just stated a fact, plenty of time to think about it, nevertheless when he returned I managed to ask in a concerned voice 'what about the cats?'

'I thought we'd let Feckless be boarded at the vets, they'll see she gets her daily tablet.'

'She won't like it.'

'No, but a holiday would do you good.' Peter was right, I did need a holiday. I was making progress, but it was a slow progress; a large part of my day was spent resting, as yet I wasn't allowed to ride Millie, although I went to the stables and talked to her; I watched Peter saddle up and ride off; I sat in the stable yard and saw horses being led out for exercise; I observed Charlie and Di stalking birds. Heidi came to me and demanded attention; I took short walks across the fields bird watching with young Anna and her four year old sister; we counted the number of different birds we spotted - ten starlings, four magpies, eight seagulls, six sparrows, two ducks a drake, three moorhens . . . .

'We shall see many more in the spring and summer,' I told them.

'I've seen a robin.' Anna was excited. Had she really seen a robin in the middle of the field? Or was she making it up to swell the numbers? It didn't matter, she was enthusiastic and that is what really counted. I had given her a book listing native birds and visitors for Christmas, she took it with her on these excursions.

'You must be very quiet, Lucy.' Anna whispered to her sister. We discovered fox earths in a hollow on the side of a hill; mole hills too numerous to count in the field near the barn, and other exciting things. It was a nature walk. All this was interesting, I was pleased to be there, but how I longed to get on Millie's back.

'Tom and Poorly Puss,' I queried. 'Do they go into a cattery?'

'No, they'll be happier at home providing Margaret can feed them.'

The 'Boys' go to Margaret when we are out; they sit on her doorstep, look in the glass fronted door and generally let it be known they are on their own. Yes, they should be all right. I am not so sure about Feckless. There followed days of studying glossy brochures; in our minds we visited several different countries, the climate was pleasant, the hotel looked comfortable, the location appealing, what about the flight? Oh no, a night flight arriving in the early hours of the morning. No good. 'What about this one?'

'No flight from our local airport,' and so it went on. Finally we found a holiday which covered all the things we were looking for, a holiday in Sardinia, neither of us had been there before; Peter booked it. Now we have three months to wait until the beginning of June, the date of the holiday. The horse will be turned out to grass, no need to worry about the mare. Three months for the weather to improve here, the 'Boys' shouldn't object to being outside, besides, they will have access to their night quarters; three months for me to feel ready for the journey. I began to warm to the idea. But would Feckless pine?

In the meantime another problem has arisen to perturb me. I have recently read that cat thieves are on the increase. A charity studying the loss and theft of family pets estimates thousands of cats are stolen each year to supply the trade in domestic cat fur. Germany is the country where demand is the greatest. As the police are not obliged to act over a missing cat without proof it has been stolen it is difficult to stamp out this growing business, especially as dead cats can be obtained from the RSPCA and it is not illegal to skin a dead cat. Will our two cats be safe at night if we leave them at home? The Cats Protection League reports seeing pets being snatched in North West London, and Petwatch, another organization, claims that as many as one hundred and fifty cats a month are being killed in South Tyneside. How can we avert this practice? I am afraid I haven't got the answer. Perhaps more vigilence by neighbours? Perhaps by forming a neighbourhood watch for pets? I think all cat lovers and owners should be alerted to this danger, which is not new.

Cruelty to animals is also on the increase. Britain has long been recognized as a nation of animal lovers, yet statistics show that animal cruelty is increasing in every single region in England and Wales. The trouble is our present laws are inadequate to protect animals; the poor cat doesn't stand a dog's chance, for the law says a person has to be convicted of cruelty to cats twice before they can be disqualified from keeping one. But a change may be on the way, an unopposed first reading has just been given to a private members Bill which should help to curb animal abuse. How can a country build a tunnel for toads to cross a main road and yet fail to protect its cats?

Meanwhile, Tom is playing with a leaf in the garden. It blows away as he rushes around in all directions in an endeavour to catch it. When he succeeds he clasps it between his front paws proceeds to roll on his back, brings his hind legs up and pounds away at the leaf still held tight by his forepaws. He can be as playful as a kitten, but don't be tempted to tickle his tummy when he rolls over, if you do, one paw, with open claws, will shoot out as swift as an arrow to draw blood on an unsuspecting arm or hand. He hasn't learned how to play gently; games with the human race are unfamiliar joys; abandoned when young he is slow to appreciate the good things in life. It took a long time before I could stroke his head or run my hand along his back. He is still shy, and very suspicious. I don't think he would go off with strangers. Poorly Puss would; any little attention goes to his head; just talking to him makes him roll over, I'm sure his lovely thick coat would be very attractive to cat thieves. But I must think positively, Peter has booked the holiday.

"His lovely thick coat would be very attractive to cat thieves"

CHAPTER 21

THE THINKER

Michael, my brother has just acquired another kitten, it turned up when snow lay on the ground and wouldn't be persuaded to leave, of course, it was given food and remained part of the household.   Michael spends much time away from home, when he returns the kitten sits by his chair gazing up at him as if he is trying to decide if my brother is part of the household;   for this reason he has been called 'The Thinker'.   Last week a four legged animal of another breed raced at Cheltenham and won the Gold Cup.   He was also called 'The Thinker'.   No, my brother did not win a hefty sum for he failed to notice The Thinker was running. Snow was falling heavily as the riders circled the parade ring; the race was delayed twice, finally it took place eighty minutes late, the softer ground which the snow produced suited The Thinker, who won with final odds of 13-2.   He had started the day, before the snow, at 14-1.

Are cats capable of thinking?   I am sure Feckless is. When she sees me with a grooming brush and an anti-flea canister in my hand she hides at once;   her little brain has told her what I intend to do with the objects in my hand; if I go to the cupboard where they are stored she rushes off to the most inaccessible place she can find.   Since Poorly Puss associates grooming with pleasure, no hiding in corners or under chairs for him.   Tom, on the other hand, is very nervous of any object in my hand;   he has an ingrained fear of being hit by anything I am holding, even a duster;   he escapes outside to make distance between us his safety barrier.   Feckless is the most intelligent of the three;   she also has appealing feminine ways of making herself admired by all.   Poorly Puss does his best by rolling over.   Tom's endearing habit is to foreshorten his body, he arches his back whilst holding his tail erect;   this display is put on when he anticipates a tasty morsel coming his way, it conveys an air of expectancy tinged with shyness.

What is the life span of a cat? A beautiful, long haired cat was shown on television the other night having just died at the marvellous age of twenty-three. I wonder if that is a record? The twenty-three year old was a master mouse catcher, having caught thousands of mice in Tyneside during his long life. I roughly estimate Feckless to be fourteen years old, Poorly Puss about ten years old and Tom much younger, possibly only six. Hopefully we shall still enjoy a good few years of their companionship. Cats need plenty of affection and company, preferring human companionship to feline; I hope we supply sufficient affection and companionship for ours - we certainly try.

There are twenty-five houses in the road where we live, from one intersection to another. I have tried to count the number of cats in this section that are known to me - I make the total fourteen. I didn't knock on doors to enquire if such and such a cat lives there, but have noted them sitting on doorsteps or on cars parked in the house drives. It is interesting to note how far each cat roams; some do not cross the road at all but mark their territory in rear gardens. Others are bolder and venture many houses away; only a few frequent our garden. Recently Jemima from across the road has taken to chasing the squirrels in our garden; she sits for hours waiting patiently at the bottom of a tree for an unsuspecting squirrel to run down from the lofty height, then a hectic chase takes place. Although I believe she is one of Poorly Puss's off-spring she in no way resembles him, having a short coat with quite startling black and white markings. I have yet to witness how Tom treats her.

Anyone who studies cats will have noticed how long it takes them to settle down; they turn at least a couple of times, often ending up where they were originally, before finally settling down on a chair or in front of the fire; it is almost as if a ritual has to be performed 'twice round for luck,' 'three times for a good nap.' I read somewhere that this habit was a legacy from their wild days when a bed in the open of bracken or twigs was made softer by turning about two or three times.

The earliest records of domesticated cats are to be found in Egypt; cats were tamed there thirteen centuries before Christ. The ancient Egyptians regarded the cat with superstitious awe and when a cat died it was embalmed and buried like a human being, members of the family even went into mourning. Mummified cats have been unearthed among the ruins of ancient Egypt. To kill a cat was a terrible crime, punishable by death. I believe the Egyptian wild cat is still to be found over a wide area in Africa, the resemblance to the domestic cat being sufficiently close to suggest a common origin. Beautiful bronze and pottery cats have survived the centuries to be admired not only by cat lovers but by all who admire things of beauty.

It is often said that whatever the Americans are doing we in England will soon copy. I hope the latest trend will not reach our shores; namely the death penalty for felines caught raiding or attacking birds. Two States have already decreed the death penalty now a third is engaged in a battle over legalising the slaughter of cats which attack birds. If American juries exonerate homeowners who shoot burglars first and ask questions later, what chance has the humble cat? I believe the wave of attacks by cats has been on geese and ducks raised for profit; one can feel sorry for the farmers concerned yet at the same time hope they will come up with another means of protecting their birds other than by shooting the cats.

There is a bird in North America which has been named after the cat; it is called the catbird; so named because of it's success in imitating the plaintive mewing of a cat in distress. These clever birds are about nine inches long; both male and female have blue-grey feathers set off by a black cap and tail, with just a touch of rust underneath the tail. They are closely related to mocking-birds. What a pity ducks and geese cannot imitate the cat!

"He never left her side"

CHAPTER 22

PADDY AND THE WAYWARD THREE

Spring has arrived.   I know because Tom has been sunning himself on the sun lounge roof.   The first time he made his way up there he gave me quite a fright; I was reading in the sun lounge when I heard a noise which sounded like human footsteps in the room above, accompanied by much creaking.   I knew I was alone in the house. What should I do?   Go and investigate I told myself; I quietly climbed the stairs to the bedroom; of course, I found no-one there.   Looking out of the window to the sun lounge roof I observed Tom turning round in circles before settling down in the warmest spot.   I returned to my reading - how silly of me not to suspect one of the cats.   Every time Tom moved the noise was incredible.   Now, in warm weather, he has chosen this as his favourite snoozing place; when it gets too hot he merely moves to one corner which is shaded by over hanging branches from our huge beech tree.

Feckless has a penchant for the inside of cardboard boxes; they never fail to intrigue her.   Whenever I return with shopping in a cardboard box, which is usual when I buy quantities of tinned cat food, she cannot wait to get inside it;   then she proceeds to scratch a corner of the box in mock battle; if she manages to tear off a piece of cardboard she rolls on her back to attack the strip with her four feet pummeling the air; suddenly she jumps out and rushes from the kitchen only to return immediately to repeat the performance, as if her very life depended upon it.

Before we had Poorly Puss neutered, (he doesn't respond to being called Rumpole) Peter built various shelters for him in the front garden.   I've already mentioned one which was cleverly hidden under a rhododendron bush next to the front door.   We lined it with old sweaters which constantly had to be replenished for they got wet when he

81

crept in during rainstorms, his long coat soaked on the outer surface. Peter covered the wooden box with thick polythene to keep it waterproof. Before we went to bed we would open the front door and softly call his name; more often than not we were rewarded by the sound of crackling leaves as Poorly Puss emerged to receive his last feed for the night.

'Peter, the dogs are roaming the street.'

'Which way are they heading?'

'They're about to enter our front garden. Are the cats inside?'

I dislike dogs roaming in a pack - if three can be called a pack, but these three in particular are a great nuisance. They charge into the gardens of all the houses in our road, barking with excitement, intent on chasing any cat in sight. One, an Alsation, lives at the top of the road; any entreaties on our behalf for the dog to be kept in unless accompanied by an adult have not been met with a favourable reply.

'She gets out of the garden so there's nothing we can do.' We have been informed. The Alsation is allowed to run after boys on their bicycles and she is allowed to make a nuisance of herself when young boys and girls deliver newspapers. Poorly Puss moves less swiftly now, jumping on to the fence is like tackling an Olympic size obstacle course, so naturally I am concerned on his behalf. A golden Labrador and a biscuit coloured cross breed make up the pack; these two call on the Alsation for the specific purpose of enticing her to hunt cats with them. I don't think the Labrador and the mongrel are local dogs; both wear collars but I do not wish to attempt to identify them when they are chasing cats. When they are not chasing cats we do not see them.

Our cats are not entirely free from being chased by a dog when they are in the rear garden, for Paddy, a Jack Russell lives in the house facing our garden, and Paddy can get over the fence. Occasionally excited barking will arouse us in the early morning; on going outside it's not unusual to find Poorly Puss on the roof of the boiler house, Tom inside with Paddy rushing up and down knowing he has got them cornered. His owners keep two cats but Paddy doesn't bother to chase them; often when I am sending him home I see their lovely tabby cat sitting quietly on the fence observing Paddy's antics. Sometimes a row of children's faces appears over the top of the fence calling Paddy home. I ask them how they manage to look over the fence which is at least six feet high.

'We're standing on bricks,' they reply. 'That's how Paddy gets over.' It is more difficult to get him back; we have no bricks our side of the fence; Paddy has to be enticed on to the compost heap from which a jump and a lot of scrambling enables him to reach the top of the fence. Paddy is small enough to leave this neighbour's house via the cat flap. The dogs will be a minor cause for concern whilst we are on holiday.

'I am sure the cats will be all right.' Peter sounds convinced. 'We can't molly-coddle them all the time.'

'True - besides the cats have always managed to escape.' So far . . . .

I decided to weigh Feckless and Tom, having re-weighed Poorly Puss to discover his weight had increased to 12 lbs. I gathered Feckless in my arms; she was lying on one of the beds, one which lies next to a radiator, not that it was giving any heat out, but she is ever hopeful; she at once started squeaking and squalling, telling me she did not want to be picked up.

'It's all right, Feckless, I'm only going to weigh you,' I cooed into her ear. Whereupon I carried her into the bath-room and stood on the scales. Feckless peered down puzzled; this was something new to her; what on earth is this all about, she seemed to be thinking. The figures on the scales are not too clear for I've had the scales a long time.

'Can you read it Peter? Feckless is obscuring my vision.' Peter got down on his hands and knees to get an accurate reading.

'Deducting your weight, 7 lbs.' he replied.

'I think that's adequate, after all she's a small cat.   I think I'll weigh Tom downstairs.'   I released Feckless who rushed to safety under a bed, no doubt thinking I had other plans for her.

Peter put the scales in the dining-room;   Tom was in his bed.   Like Feckless, Tom dislikes being picked up.

'We shall have to read this quickly,' I said, anticipating trouble with Tom.   Tom was suspicious of me getting hold of him, he started struggling immediately;   I got on the scales which oscillated with the movement in my arms.

'Keep still!'   Peter commanded.

'I can't.   Read it quickly.'

'Nearly 10 lbs. no 10½ lbs. - no 10 lbs.'

With an enormous heave Tom leapt from my arms to hasten to the back door.

'Why didn't you put them in the travelling basket and stand that on the scales?   It would have been a lot easier.' Peter mildly rebuked me for being unpractical.

'The cats would have thought they were going some-where unpleasant.   Anyway, mission accomplished!'

CHAPTER 23

THREE ORDINARY CATS

'Why not check Millie's weight, see if she's lost condition through the winter?' Peter suggested.

'She looks too fat to me,' I answered, 'but all right, we'll measure her to-day.'

The way to obtain the body weight of a horse, unless you put it on a weighbridge, and where does the everyday horse owner find a weighbridge?, is to take a measurement round the horse's girth (round the barrel). Several horse feed manufacturers make charts available giving estimated bodyweights according to the size of the girth. So if the girth measures seventy-two inches the horse's estimated weight is 1100 lbs. Ideally regular measurements should be taken in order to judge whether the level of feeding should be adjusted. Another reason for needing to know how much your horse weighs is in the administration of worming granules or pastes. My mare needs two packets of worming granules or one full syringe of worming paste, for she weighs roughly 1200 lbs.

We arrived at the stables after lunch; Millie was looking out of her stable watching everything going on in the yard. I removed her rugs (it is still cold at night so she is wearing two rugs), and put the tape measure round her. In fact it is two tape measures joined together, I haven't yet got round to buying one specially designed for equines. Millie turned her head to sniff the tape measure. 'She's increased an inch.' I exclaimed.

'I shouldn't worry about an inch, that's only 10 lbs,' Peter replied.

Last winter Millie lost condition. I called the vet for

85

she was showing poverty lines down her quarters; I could see her ribs too clearly and her coat looked dull.

'There's no goodness in the hay,' the vet informed me.

'Last summer's crop was poor due to the wet weather. She needs to graze good grass and to feel the sun on her back.'

It was difficult at that precise time of the year because John was resting his fields and all the horses were stabled. The vet put her on a vitamin supplement and I led her out to graze the grass verges whenever possible. As soon as the horses were turned into the fields she looked a different animal. Determined to avoid a repetition the following winter I started Millie on a vitamin supplement in November. She has come through the winter with flying colours; her coat shines, her eyes are bright and the spring in her step together with a thin layer of fat over her ribs all denote a healthy horse.

Di decided to see what was going on; she jumped on the stable door and met Millie's startled gaze as the mare lowered her head to sniff the intruder. 'Off you go Di, you might get trodden on in here.' I pushed the cat gently off the door; not at all put out she wandered round the corner of the stable block in search of other amusements.

The sun was shining; Peter saddled up. 'She looks well,' I said. 'Her summer coat is coming through.' I watched him leave the well swept yard, then I took a book out of the car and settled down in a warm corner to wait their return. I was in two minds, should I walk across the fields in the hope of seeing the birds with curved beaks I noticed yesterday? The fields would be very muddy, water covered the lower lying ones so that small lakes were visible. John was again resting the fields for the horses would soon poach the ground when it was in this condition, then the grazing for the summer would be ruined. Were the birds two curlews? Peter's binoculars were not in the car yesterday, it was difficult to be sure with the naked eye; the birds had not given the haunting cry of the curlew, but then they had been busy feeding in the water filled field. Young Anna would have liked to watch them, but she was in bed with a sore throat so I had been unable to share my discovery with her. Coots had found the wet fields to their liking. 'Don't get silly ideas about nesting,' I told them. 'This field will be quite different in a few weeks' time.' A heron flew over as we drove up the drive to-day; it alighted by a natural pond made even deeper by the recent rain. 'No fish in there,' I murmured. He must have heard me, for one brief moment he was a tall silhouette, the next a huge bird in the sky flapping his wings effortlessly. I had my rubber boots with me so I could venture down there, but it would be hard work pulling each leg out of squelchy mud. No, I would read the book I had taken with me.

My thoughts wandered to the three cats at home. Tom and Poorly Puss had been put in the garden when we left - Feckless had the whole house to herself. On such occasions she likes to go into the dining-room to sit on the window-sill until we return. When she hears the car she hides under a chair in the hall, waiting until the 'Boys' have come in, then she asks to be let out in the rear garden. The hall gets busy as Poorly Puss pushes in first then turns round to prevent Tom from entering. Yesterday I gathered up the big fellow in my arms and told Tom to come in - Poorly Puss retaliated by grabbing hold of my arm and scratching me. I scolded him, whereupon he retreated to the kitchen with a very angry look on his normally angelic face.

'Now 'Boys' don't fight.' They don't fight all the time, sometimes they greet each other touching faces then sit patiently waiting to be fed. Occasionally Feckless watches them having positioned herself on the bottom stair, ready to rush upstairs if Tom comes too close to her. If I follow upstairs Feckless dashes ahead to a bedroom, begging me to play with her, or jumps on a bed making little mewing sounds, as if to say 'stay with me awhile.' I call out to Peter 'I've been waylaid by Feckless,' as I stop to give her the attention she demands.

Glancing out of the dining-room window the other day I noticed Poorly Puss sitting in the garage drive of the house opposite; he was flanked by Jasper and Jemima - his off-spring. 'Try to get a photograph,' I called to Peter; I knew his camera was in the car. Poorly Puss heard the car door being opened and walked across the road to Peter. I wonder if he is aware of the relationship? The three cats sitting quietly together made a pretty family group.

My thoughts become more serious. I am due to see the consultant in a week's time. What joy if it were to be my last visit! Will he declare me fit to ride my mare? I become apprehensive, then dismissing unwelcome thoughts I remind myself how much I have enjoyed writing about the cats in my life whilst forced to rest. I dare say I have forgotten one or two - memory is not infallible. In the main this narrative has concentrated on three seemingly ordinary cats, but three who have brought a little magic into our lives for each cat makes us happy in a different way, as each one delights and pleases us in the way it knows best. I would not wish to part with Tom, Poorly Puss or the little black lady, the loveable Queen Feckless. How can I call them 'Just Cats'?